The Journal of the Three Days of the Battle of Waterloo

The Journal of the Three Days of the Battle of Waterloo

An Account of the Campaign of 1815
From Within the French Army

An Eyewitness

LEONAUR

The Journal of the Three Days of the Battle of Waterloo
An Account of the Campaign of 1815
From Within the French Army
by an Eyewitness

First published under the title
The Journal of the Three Days of the Battle of Waterloo

Leonaur is an imprint
of Oakpast Ltd

ISBN: 978-0-85706-341-0 (hardcover)
ISBN: 978-0-85706-342-7 (softcover)

http://www.leonaur.com

Contents

Publisher's Introduction

Not long before the publication of the Leonaur edition of this book, *The Journal of the Three Days of the Battle of Waterloo*, the Leonaur editors were in the city of Paris, combining business with a little pleasure. They had emerged from the Pantheon—the merits of this beautiful building need no elaboration here—where the great men and women of France are commemorated or incarcerated. For one of the Leonaur editors this was something of a regular pilgrimage that had begun over forty years previously, and which concerned architecture hardly at all.

At the age of fourteen he made the acquaintance of the great mural, painted by Edouard Detaille, which is the focal point of the Pantheon's interior, sited as it is directly opposite its principal entrance. It is an allegorical work which romantically portrays the spirit warriors of the legions of Revolution, Consulate and Empire bearing the captured banners of their vanquished foes in a whirlwind up to heaven and under the approving gaze of Winged Victory. The first sight of this inspiring piece of propaganda impacted on this future editor's young sensibilities in much the manner, one may suppose, the artist intended it should on everyone who looked upon it.

This initial acquaintance, since regularly renewed, also promoted a lifelong interest in military history, military illustration and art and the work of Monsieur Detaille in particular. The rest, as they say, is history—in this case quite literally!

As the editors paused on the *portico* enjoying the sunshine, at the end of the avenue before them, the dome of Napoleons tomb could be seen gleaming warmly beyond the trees of the Luxembourg Gardens and they conferred as to where should be their next destination. Would it be another notable sight of the French capital or the nearest bistro?

Inspired by the view, the editors decided upon another experience of Parisian culture (after a cold beer) when they were approached by a French gentleman who addressed them in excellent English. Cordially, he enquired if they had enjoyed their experience within and was informed that they had. By way of conversation, the story of this 'pilgrimage' was also imparted to the French gentleman and although he was too polite to be judgemental, it came as a small surprise when he gave the impression that as reasons to visit the Pantheon go, a viewing of Detaille's mural was not, in his unelaborated opinion, an especially good one. This was something of a dampener for one stricken by hero worship when it comes to Detaille's talent.

"And where," he then enquired, "are you planning to go next?"

Sensing that complete honesty might not be the best policy at this point, one of the editors decided to skip reference to the immediate intention and pointing down the Rue Soufflot told him that we were going to the military museum at Les Invalides and, of course, Napoleon's tomb which is adjacent to it. Alas, honesty might have been preferable, as once again he seemed unimpressed. He had apparently decided that we were the victims of some kind of misguidance.

"We are *not*," he said with Gallic emphasis, "too impressed with *this* Napoleon, we French!"

The implication of this renunciation was so evident it almost seemed he had said '*your*' Napoleon!

This came as something of a revelation to three foreigners in Paris where the Carrousel stands by the Louvre which in turn is adorned with statues of Napoleon's marshals and generals, where the Arc de Triomphe, visible for miles, presides at the end of the Champs Elysees, where monuments, bridges, streets and squares recall his victories and his great men, where the 'N' is omnipresent and where the man himself lies at rest within a sarcophagus under a golden dome that would impress a pharaoh—and we told the French gentleman so. As *rationales* go this one was also considered poor. He correctly pointed out that the man himself, in all his hubris, was responsible for much, if not all, of *that* and what were the French people to do now—demolish it all?

"*History* is, after all, *history*," he said, "and could not be undone. Now Bonaparte," he continued with obvious affection and pride, "there is man we have loved!"

This is not a totally unfamiliar view of a dual personality, but it is an uncommon one. Very rarely can we make such a clear distinction in the character of a single human being. Possibly the name change assists, as in the case of the fictional *nice* Dr. Jekyll and *evil* Mr Hyde. Clearly neither one could be responsible for the behaviour of the other, but usually in real life, after a fall in public estimation, the only person who fondly recalls the individual's alleged good points is his own mother and everyone else attributes this is to understandable delusion.

Since the Leonaur Editors are not French, it is difficult to judge whether this gentleman's view of their former Emperor is widely held among French people or is peculiarly his own. It is also difficult to reconcile this gentleman's view with our own Anglo-Saxon cultural sentiment in which when a *good name* is lost it is forever beyond redemption. Of course, only the French are in possession of their past and no doubt there is much divided opinion on this gentleman's view as there is on many other subjects.

It is some 200 years or more since the age of Napoleon, depending upon how one wishes to benchmark it. Of course, the Leonaur editors know what that French gentleman meant. He was making a clear distinction, possibly too clear if dispassionate truth be told, between the Bonaparte of the Revolution and Consulate and the Emperor Napoleon of the First Empire. The time elapsed between the age of Napoleon and the present day can be judged, according to one's interpretation, either as an age of crucial importance or as so insignificant in historical terms as to be irrelevant. But what is significant about it, within the context of this introduction, is that the French gentleman's view is demonstrably shared by the anonymous author of the book you are now holding which was written soon after the final fall of Napoleon in 1815. The parallels seemed so clear as to be noteworthy.

There are several accounts of the Napoleonic period which at the time of their original publication withheld, for a variety of reasons, the identity of their authors from readers. Their covers simply attributed the author as *Anonymous*, or as in this case *An Eyewitness*. Research by historians has in some cases revealed the identities of previously anonymous authors, and Leonaur has been fortunate enough to be able to include these on several books previously anonymously published. So we have come learn of James Todd,[1] John Hering,[2] Thomas Garrety[3] and several others who were once *unknown*.

It could therefore be that the identity of the author of this book is known to someone, but we have to admit that our own considerable investigations have failed to reveal it; so, to learn more about him, we must embark on the perilous and, perhaps, unreliable path of deduction based on what we believe we can glean from the authors own words.

The text you are about to read is a translation from the original French and, in our view, could not, even in that language, have borne a version of its English title, for within these pages the great battle is not referred to as the Anglicised *Waterloo*, a designation even Wellington's Prussian allies did not use, but more plausibly as *Mont St. Jean*. Its presentation is only nominally that of a journal, since it contains information that could only have been available after the event, including details of a wide spread of actions that one involved could not possibly have witnessed. In fact, much within these pages could potentially have been

---

1. *Bayonets, Bugles and Bonnets* by James 'Thomas' Todd, published by Leonaur.
2. *Journal of an Officer in the King's German Legion* by John Frederick Hering, published by Leonaur.
3. *Soldiering With the 'Division'* by Thomas Garrety, published by Leonaur.

derived from third party sources.

That is not to imply the Leonaur editors doubt the authenticity of the text. Sir Walter Scott was apparently much impressed with this work and used it as source material and inspiration for his great poem on the Battle of Waterloo. In fairness, however, Scott's name does not by its fame alone bestow any additional credibility to this text and he may have been impressed with this less had he had at his disposal the volume of material on the battle published after this account and now available to present day students and readers.

The author tells us that he is a gentleman. The book certainly is the work of a well educated man and it was written at a time when higher education was a privilege few enjoyed and those who did enjoy it paid for it at their own expense. So given the style of the authors prose and his grasp of political and social matters we must assume this to be true.

The author styles himself a *soldier* and this is plausible. He gives us opinions and states his position on matters from his emphasised position *as a soldier*. That he thought of himself primarily as a soldier would also suggest that he was not new to the profession. In his descriptions of the actions of the French army as a participant he uses the word *we* which suggests he was one of their number. His understanding of strategy, grand tactics and tactics and the dispositions of troops underlines not only his education and social standing, born out by his claim to be a *gentleman*, but may also tends to suggest that he was an officer.

Much of the author's writing suggests, with the single exception of his view of the Prussians, an intellectual ability to be even handed. He clearly despises the Prussians at every level, from their aristocrats to their generals to their abilities as soldiers. Indeed, he makes it clear, that in his opinion had the campaign of 1815 been simply a matter of dealing with the Prussian Army, without the telling influence of the British—whom he believes to be of a different calibre, the outcome would have been an easy French victory. Whether that is true or not is moot, but it suggests that the author had, in his capacity as a soldier, encountered the Prussian army in the past with some success—or had some other experience of them that made a dispassionate opinion impossible for him.

It is difficult to ascertain to which branch of the army the author may have been attached. He does not appear to have been sufficiently close to Napoleon to have been part of the staff. His references to the artillery or the cavalry display no particular intimacy. He describes the attitudes of the Imperial Guard with a clear tone of censure. He seems to have considered them as Napoleon's *zealots* who thought themselves unreasonably *a cut above* the rest of the army and whose behaviour to other French soldiers was reprehensible, so it is probable that he was not one of their number.

The author makes clear reference to the departure of Grouchy from the main army, but the reader has no impression that the he moves with that wing of the campaign. This suggests that the author was present on the principal battlefield. References are sparse, but the Leonaur Editors feel that it in the description of the great infantry attacks in column—*as we labour our feet through the cloying impeding mud of the valley to the Allied centre*—that the writer's own experience seems most compelling. So dare we suggest he may have been an experienced infantry officer of the French line regiments?

The most intriguing aspect of the author's account is embodied in his loyalty to and approval (or otherwise) of those whose cause he served, irrespective of his own feelings. In this he displays what we may consider to be the position of a modern soldier. He makes it clear that he believes the role of the army is to be in service to those who are the legitimate government at the time. He emphasises that anyone who had given their oaths to the restored Bourbon king had no business to be on the field at Waterloo (Mont St. Jean). In fact he goes so far as to name such people traitors. So he clearly held many of the prominent military figures of the Napoleonic period in very low regard by this time. Yet there he was in the ranks of Napoleon's army. This seems to suggest that he had made no such oath himself. This might be easily explained if he had resigned from the army after the fall of Napoleon, in whose service he had clearly learned his trade, and then rallied to the Emperor on his return from Elba; but perhaps not if he had remained in the army after the restoration unless he was able to do so without specific undertakings as to his own personal position. If he was able to effect this transition by keeping his own council that might suggest he was not a particularly senior officer.

Clearly his presence on the field of conflict reveals him to be no ardent royalist which is unsurprising. The Bourbons had not ruled France for over two decades of the authors life and their record as far as anyone who had no vested interest in them was concerned was a poor one. Any doubts on that score are quickly dispelled when the author declares that *he will never acknowledge the rights of kings, but such as they have been derived from the people.*

Yet by the same token he *abhors Jacobites*, condemns the *anarchy* of the revolution, believes that Louis the 16th was *savagely murdered* and also asserts at the time of the restoration that Louis the 18th was France's *legitimate king.*

Likewise the author believes that Bonaparte fulfilled the hopes of the French people and nation, and, significantly, like his modern day counterpart on the Pantheon steps, he also uses the exact distinction of change of character with change of appellation. He even acknowledges Napoleon's right to become emperor, but then condemns him for what he became—in his view a despot—and what he brought upon the nation thereafter; so he was no blind follower of Napoleon. Here is a man who accepts that authority is essential, but believes that this can never be separated from moral responsibility, irrespective of title or birthright, and in this we see the key to the man.

Given that some of the foregoing analysis is correct, perhaps we can begin to understand why the author elected to remain anonymous. He finds himself unable to subscribe to the views, without caveats, of any of the principal factions engaged in the tumultuous events of which he is a part. He even suggests that the behaviour of the French army in the field did much to bring about the misfortunes that the French nation ultimately suffered, and in that regard they had, perhaps, reaped no more than the bitter harvest they had sown. It is not difficult to see that this is a man who would struggle to be popular in any camp of his day, other than that of his own principles. His decision to hide his identity may therefore be more a case of prudence being the better part of valour, except within the anonymity of his written words.

In the tone of the account generally, assuming the absence of hypocrisy, there has to be a reason why the author of this book marched towards the lines of Wellington's waiting guns. So we should seek evidence of this reason in the text.

Quite simply, France was about to be invaded. Foreign armies and their soldiery were about to set foot on French soil and impose themselves upon French people in French villages and towns. What was a French soldier to do under such circumstances? Irrespective of who or what had brought this about the *die had been cast*, it was now the responsibility and duty of the soldiers of France to do their part to defend the nation. If Napoleon could provide the inspiration for this task then that was his principal benefit at that moment. It is a short term philosophy, but perhaps a reasonable one when the *enemy is at the gate*.

So our author was above all a patriot—a true Frenchman—and we can only admire the simple philosophy that prompted him to risk his life for that quintessential principle. He was, of course, a product of his time and despite his belief in serving the legitimate government of his country he inevitably saw that from the perspective of a free thinking person confident in his right to consider and make judgements on the issues that concerned him. He was essentially a republican, and like so many French people of his time (and since) would ever have the sensibilities of a *citizen* regardless of any other consideration. Nothing else would be acceptable to him, the revolution had done its indelible work and, irrespective of any perversions, the basic principles which drove it resound to this day. Such change, having been embraced by a people, is all but impossible reverse, nothing will coerce or force them to surrender their rights. If we subscribe to this hypothesis we can see the course of French history beyond the time of Napoleon to the present day—and perhaps onto the steps of the Pantheon and within to the names of those inscribed there. France honours those who serve France and is *not too impressed* with those who serve only themselves and use the French people to do it. In Bonaparte our author saw a great leader of the French nation by the terms of his republican sensibilities, whereas in Napoleon he saw one who used the nation for his own egomaniacal ends.

Even Marbot,[1] whose adoration of his emperor approached the ludicrous heights of his fictional counterpart, Conan Doyle's Brigadier Gerard,[2] referred, in his substantial autobiography of life under the eagles, to Napoleon's *evil genius*, so making it clear, as does the author of this book, that he knew his master for what he was—a military mastermind without parallel (though one no longer in possession of his former talents) but ultimately and above all a monster. What is perhaps most astonishing to some of us is that there are those who over time are able retrospectively, by their appreciation of the magnitude and brilliance of one aspect of the Bonaparte-Napoleon character, to tolerate the worst excesses of the other.

Our French gentleman of the Pantheon portico apparently feels the same way, and it is perhaps now not difficult to understand why. All the pomp and pageantry created around Napoleon was, of course, designed to disguise the fundamental truth from examination—not for the first or last time—by diversions of the most insubstantial kind; it worked for a time. It is understandable then, that this realisation may encourage some to put little value on them now. The Leonaur editors also appreciate

---

1. Marbot's autobiography is published in three volumes by Leonaur: *The Life of the Real Brigadier Gerard Volume 1 The Young Hussar 1782-1807, The Life of the Real Brigadier Gerard Volume 2 Imperial Aide-De-Camp 1807-1811 & The Life of the Real Brigadier Gerard Volume 3 Colonel Of Chasseurs 1811-1815.*
2. All of Conan Doyle's Brigadier Gerard stories are available in a single volume Leonaur edition, that for the first time includes all the original magazine illustrations: *The Illustrated & Complete Brigadier Gerard.*

that though Detaille painted in the service of another Napoleon, much of his work, in its way, was put to the same purpose as its equivalent in the time of the First Empire.

Despite that we still think Detaille painted beautiful pictures!

The Leonaur Editors

Personal Journal, &c.

*June 13,*1815.—The French nation is degraded (let it be confessed) by the eager servitude with which all classes are seeking to recommend themselves to the restored king. There are rights of kings; be it so, but are there not rights of the people likewise? Louis the 16th was most savagely murdered by the Jacobins of that day. I allow it; no one can more execrate that murder than myself. A most horrible anarchy succeeded, and was only terminated when Buonaparte arrived from Egypt, and became Consul. France then beheld that he fulfilled her hopes; his government was firm and vigorous; he subdued domestic factions and conquered peace.

It was then put to the vote throughout France,—Shall Napoleon become Emperor of the French? The Nation (it becomes the honour of military men to be direct, open, and true), the Nation, I say, gave their votes by acclamation, that Napoleon had deserved well of the French people, and should therefore be their Emperor. Such was his title, and who will deny that it was legitimate,—the undoubted voice and choice of the people during a vacant throne. Napoleon therefore was Emperor of the French. An unhappy, or to speak with the same candour, a most atrocious career of ambition and despotism then seized upon the Emperor, and the vengeance of heaven awakened by so much, blood, precipitated him into the abyss of misfortunes; he abdicated his throne and withdrew into exile.

Louis the 18th was then placed upon the throne; the people received him, and he thereby became their legitimate king. The return of Napoleon was a breach of treaty both with France and with the other nations of Europe. The allied armies, therefore, as far as Napoleon was concerned, had a good right of war; and as Napoleon had already abdicated his original fight, and France had acquired new obligations, it was a clear and decided treason in Frenchmen to desert Louis, and to go over to Napoleon. This is my political confession of faith, and upon this I have acted.—

Napoleon was Emperor till he abdicated. Louis is now the lawful sovereign because he was received as such by the French people upon the crown being thus vacated. I abhor Jacobinism; but upon the honour of a gentleman, and upon the faith of a soldier, I never have, and never will acknowledge any right in kings, but such as they have derived from the people.

But let me proceed to the subject upon which I regard it my duty to relate what I know and saw. I was present in that memorable and fatal battle which will bear a prominent part in our annals to the end of time. As far as my humble talents can avail, neither faction, nor a meaner spirit of flattery, shall give any false colour. I pretend not to History, but to Testimony. I will relate what I saw—let others adorn.

This day the Emperor and his immediate staff left Paris for the army. The hopes and fears of the French, almost in equal division, went with him. Let me briefly explain. The sudden appearance of Buonaparte in France was a thunderbolt to all the honourable portion of the French people,—in a word, to all those who had the good and tranquillity of their country at heart. What in fact could be expected to result from it but a foreign and civil war, devouring and ravaging everything before it

But unhappily a concourse of unfortunate circumstances ensured the success of this fatal enterprise. Who will believe, that this extraordinary man, who had so long oppressed all Europe and his own country, had still so many adherents,—had still so many ready and welcoming friends, as mad and no less wicked than himself.

The army were almost to a man in his favour Almost to a man they betrayed their oaths to the, best of kings, and carrying their perfidy even to, the point of turning their arms against him, they compelled him to abandon his capital. All well-disposed Frenchmen had thus the grief of seeing Buonaparte not only make his way to Paris, but of seeing him enter it as if in triumph.

He returned to his former system with his former power. He employed every means to unite the people in his guilt and madness; he spared no means to deceive them both in his projects and resources; and he succeeded but too effectually in rendering a very considerable portion of the nation his dupe and instrument.

It is truly a matter of astonishment to what point he carried these deceptions. Not satisfied with loading with reproaches the respectable name of the king and the Bourbons,—not satisfied with awakening the apprehensions of the proprietors of national property with respect to the actual purposes of Louis XVIIIth, he announced, with, the most astonishing impudence, that he had concerted his whole enterprise with the Emperor of Austria: and as a proof of such concert, promised the immediate arrival of his son and the Empress Maria Louisa.

Confounded by these positive assertions, France began to indulge a hope that the country might yet avoid the war which Europe had menaced against her. Even the most grave and thinking men could scarcely force themselves to believe, that the Emperor Napoleon would thus grossly deceive them. On the other hand, the people, or rather the populace, were naturally dazzled by the romantic daring of the enterprise; and this enthusiasm on the one part, and the doubts on the other, ended in uniting an immense party in submission to the dynasty again produced to them. by fortune.

Proclamation now succeeded proclamation. He affected to wish only for peace, and he invoked the treaty of Paris. Under the pretext of referring his power and crown to the people, he convoked an Assembly, but of which he required no other service than that of declaring the war national. In the midst of his weakness he dreamt only of victory and conquest, and spoke of the nation only as the instrument of his vengeance and ambition. But he was scarcely upon his throne before he evinced that he was not in his proper station. Impatient to figure in his own

19

proper theatre, the field of blood and battle, he pressed with an incredible activity the reconstruction of his armies,—the levies of men and money, and the fabrication and conveyance of arms.

From all parts troops were levied, united, and dispatched towards the frontiers; the battalions were filled up with restored prisoners; with pensionaries, with new levies. The National Guards were organised. Arms of all kinds, artillery of all calibre, and equipages innumerable, seemed to issue as if by enchantment from the arsenals and foundries; and within a few days France was transformed into a vast camp. Whilst the first and that a numerous army, filed towards Belgium, others were assembled in Alsace, Lorraine, Franche Compté, on the verge of the Alps, and the Pyrenees.

In despite of the protestations of Napoleon, that he desired nothing but the maintenance of peace, the powers of Europe were too well informed in the character of that perfidious man to hesitate with respect to their policy. The Congress of Vienna issued successive declarations, in which they denominated him an outlaw in the system of Europe. They followed up these manifestoes by prohibiting all intercourse between France and their dominions, and by putting their armies in march towards our frontiers.

There was now, therefore, no farther room to hope that Austria would be induced to mediate. All Europe was again in arms to expel from his throne a man who had been replaced there only by the most atrocious perjury.

In the midst of all these movements, the deputies arrived at Paris to assist at the *Champ de Mai,* that theatrical spectacle by which this ambitious man expected to deceive a nation.. We there beheld many respectable names,—many illustrious men, who were willing to avail themselves of any chance to save their country; but amidst these unexceptionable members were, innumerable others, who were only the slaves, the tools, or the confederates of the usurper, and who having a common interest with their master had no other views or purposes than to assist in his intrigues. The result of the *Champ de Mai* was therefore such as might be expected. An additional act was most impudently published as a benefit to liberty and the constitution; an act, the substance and meaning of which were to establish a military despotism upon a popular basis; to deceive the people into the basest servitude, and to subdue liberty and the laws under the foot of its iron master.

Whilst these events were passing in the capital, the armies were daily receiving the most considerable reinforcements; and innumerable levies, from all parts of the empire, were hastening towards the appointed points of concentration upon the frontiers

The army of the north, which was the most numerous, occupied, in the beginning of June, very extended cantonments in the departments of the North and the Aisne, where it was disposed in *echellons*, The headquarters were at Laon. The first corps occupied Valenciennes, and the second Maubeuge

It communicated by its right with the army of the Ardennes and that of the Moselle; its left was appuyed upon Lille. Being constituted in its greater part of the old soldiers now restored to their country, it, was animated with the most inflexible courage and the most ardent enthusiasm towards its former leader, the Emperor Napoleon. It passed its time in the daily interchange of good offices with the inhabitants of the department of the Aisne, who regarded the war as national, and, who employed themselves, as brave and honourable Frenchmen in preparing to defend their country against the imminent invasion of foreigners. Upon all sides they fortified their cities, and covered all the roads and avenues with *têtes-de-pont*, abbatis, and field-redoubts.

The National Guards were equally forward in arming themselves. All the population expressed their resolute purpose of going forth in mass. The same spirit manifested itself in all those departments of France, which had been the theatre of war in the preceding campaign of 1814. The department of the North was a solitary exception; the inhabitants of this department expressed contrary sentiments, and its national guards refused. to march.

The army and people infact reckoned each upon the other at the moment when hostilities were about to commence.

The people believed that the allies had been enabled to invade France in 1814 only by means of successive acts of treason; they flattered themselves, therefore, that the union of the people and the soldiery would save France.

Under these circumstances, there was a general anxiety for the commencement of active operations. The army looked to the moment of battle as the moment of victory.

Such was the state of affairs, when the Imperial Guard, after having discharged its duty in the *Champ de Mai*, departed from Paris, and directed its march upon Laon. A few days after, the Emperor Napoleon himself followed this movement, and travelled with his usual rapidity towards the frontier. In reality Napoleon and his guard arrived nearly at the same hour at Vervens, where he put himself at the head of his army. The passage of troops by Vervens and Avesnes was unbroken during many successive days. It seemed as if all France was hastening to one point, and as if all were occupied with but one mind. Was this a common and unanimous enthusiasm in favour of the Emperor? No,—it was the enthusiasm of Frenchmen to defend their country against foreign invasion; and Napoleon was welcome because a suitable instrument.

A hundred victories had already declared him a conqueror. It might be wished that his civil government were more consistent with the principles of liberty and with his own frequent pledges and promises. But this was not a time to attend to these matters. Let the foreigners be expelled; let France reassume its ascendency, and the government might be amended at leisure.

Under these feelings the Emperor was everywhere received with acclamation. It is impossible to deny it.

It was at first thought, that the Emperor would not begin the attack, but would satisfy himself with taking up a long defensive line upon the frontier. But the moment of his arrival was that of the commencement of his characteristic activity; he reviewed every thing; he inspected everything; he ordered everything; he daily and hourly exhibited himself to his troops, and they hailed him with the rapture which belonged to their leader in so many wars.

Upon arriving at Beaumont, the army of the North formed its junction with that of the Ardennes, under the command of Vandamme, whose headquarters were at Furnay. The army of the Moselle, under General Girard, quitting Metz by forced marches, debouched in the same period by Phillipville, and brought itself likewise into line. Thus the army of the North was composed of five corps of infantry, under the respective commands of the Lt-Generals D'Erlon, Reille, Vandamme, Girard, and the Count de Lobau. The cavalry, commanded in-chief by Marshal Grouchy, was divided into four corps, under the orders of Generals Pajol, Excelmans, Milhaud, and Kellerman.

The Imperial Guard, which was 20,000 in strength, formed the head and point of the wedge; it was followed by a sufficient *materiel*, and there was no deficiency of every kind of equipage and appointment. Independently of the batteries attached to each division, each corps had its park of reserve. The Guard itself had a most superb train composed almost solely of new pieces.

These troops, all of them the flower of France, composed a force of nearly 150,000 men, of which 20,000 were cavalry; the artillery was not short of 300 pieces.

Already, however; even in the very bosom of their country, these troops evinced their want of that military discipline, which constitutes the strength of armies, and renders them the sure defence of the countries which they occupy. With a total disregard for their unhappy countrymen, who zealously contended to supply them with the means of subsistence, the French soldiers treated the farmers and peasantry with the most extreme rigour; and considering pillage as one of their most indisputable rights, almost made a merit of practising it in every excess.

Everywhere they sacked the houses; and under the pretext of seeking for provisions broke open the doors, committed outrages upon the inhabitants, and seized whatever suited their purposes. "We are now in the field;" said they; "we are wanted, and it is not much to allow us the ordinary license of war, the cause is not too pure; let them not demand of us, that of which they exhibit no example in themselves." Thus, going from house to house, from granary to granary, from cellar to cellar, the soldiers returned to the camp loaded with the spoils of their countrymen; and thus at one and the same moment rendered themselves unfit for war, and indisposed the country against them.

It is truly afflicting to acknowledge, that the greater part of the officers opposed only a feeble resistance to this infamous pillage, and even tolerated, if not encouraged it, under the ready excuse,—"We must not be too severe: the soldier must live. Why were there no magazines?" And whilst the soldier had his subsistence, the officer, it may be imagined, had abundance, and was only perplexed by the difficulty of choice. Do we recognize here, it may be demanded, the frank and loyal character of the French officer? No, certainly not. But let not the French name be disgraced with posterity because the officers of Buonaparte were not those of Turenne and Villeroi.

In the midst of this herd of lawless and unprincipled devastators, there were doubtless not wanting many men of honour and principle, who most grievously lamented over this frightful disorder, and who served with profound regret in this rebellious army, but who endeavoured to persuade themselves that it was their duty to defend their country under any leader. A principle of military honour kept them firm to their post They were indifferent to Napoleon but they loved France.

Nor was it, perhaps, possible to repress those disorders in an army which had been formed to them by the habit and example of twenty years. It was in fact by this system of brigandage, that the Emperor Napoleon had succeeded in so firmly attaching the soldiers to his name and cause.

The country which the army was traversing, covered with wheat already browning, promised a rich harvest: but this abundance existed in vain; woe to the fields through which was the passage of the troops; and still more so to those which became the position of a camp. In a few moments the labour and gift of the year were trodden under the feet of men and horses, or torn up by the roots for fodder.

The interior of the army was torn to pieces by an anarchy

similar to that which reigned without. It seemed as if an implacable hatred animated one corps against another, and that there existed an open war between them. No mutual sacrifices,—no reciprocal confidence, no common feeling; but every where selfishness, arrogance, and rapacity. When the commander of a column or regiment arrived at the post which he was to occupy, his first care was to seize everything within his reach, with a total disregard of anyone who might succeed him. Guards were placed at the doors of houses which contained any provisions, and without any other right than that of being the first occupant, they opposed themselves to every kind of division. These sentinels were frequently attacked by soldiers of other parties, and the matter proceeded to blows, in the course many were wounded, and some even killed, on both sides.

The Imperial Guard, in its character of being the *Janissaries* of the Despot, were extremely arrogant towards the other troops; they repelled with disdain all commerce and contact with the other branches of the service, and were justly detested by them. Their comrades submitted to this presumption only so far as the Imperial Guard were sufficiently numerous to enforce its but when they were in less number, they retaliated upon them. The different arms of cavalry were equally jealous and contentious of each other and of the infantry; whilst the latter, confident of its strength and numbers, threatened the cavalry with their bayonet, and insisted upon their own equality of rights and respect.

Such was the spirit of the army whilst on its advance towards the frontier; a spirit which rendered them as formidable to their officers as to the enemy; and which rendered it a matter of doubt to the farmers and peasantry whether their own army or that of the enemy was most to be dreaded.

The army pursued its march with the most inconceivable rapidity; the weather, though stormy, was dry, and the roads were not so much trodden as to impede the artillery and equipages. The movements were thus made with a celerity which partook of precipitation. It was now the evident hope and purpose of Napoleon to fall by surprise upon the enemy, and there was no longer any doubt with respect to the general plan of the Emperor.

June 14th.—On this day, the 14th of June, 1815 (for as every cotemporary record of this great campaign will descend to remote posterity, let me mark the date), the French army, with the Emperor Napoleon at its head, was united upon the extreme frontier, when the following proclamation, marked with the rapidity, the abruptness, and certainly the greatness of mind of the Emperor, was issued from his headquarters; and each division and regiment being duly drawn up, was read at the head of each.

Soldiers,

Behold the anniversary of Marengo and Friedland which has twice decided the destinies of Europe. It was then, as at Austerlitz, as at Wagram, that we were too generous to an enemy at our feet. We gave our easy faith to the protestations and oaths of those princes to whom we left their thrones. These same princes, having leagued amongst themselves, are now in arms against the independence of France. Let us march to give them the meeting, both they and we are still the same.

Soldiers, at Jena, against these same Prussians, we were one against three; and at Montmirail, one against six.

As many of you as have been prisoners amongst the English, relate to your comrades what you suffered in their prisons and hulks.

The Saxons, Belgians, and Hanoverians, and soldiers of the Confederation of the Rhine, lament that unhappy force which compels them to obey those princes who are the enemies of justice and liberty. They know the insatiable cupidity of this coalition. They know that these princes have already devoured twelve millions of Poles, twelve millions of Italians, a million of Saxons, and six millions of Belgians, and thus all the German states of the second order are their next destined prey.

Madmen! a moment of prosperity has blinded them. The oppression and humiliation of the French people are beyond their power; if they enter France, they will find in it only their grave.

Soldiers, we have marches to make, battles to give, and dangers to incur; but with constancy, discipline, and a resolution to conquer, the victory will be ours; and the glory and liberty of France will be reconquered.

For all Frenchman who have a heart, the moment is come to conquer or to die.

It is totally unnecessary to add, that this proclamation, thus addressed to the national and military feeling of Frenchmen, was received with the most rapturous acclamations, and that every one promised themselves victory under such a leader. Alas that his talents ware not seconded by his virtues! The French Princes of Bourbon have themselves lamented this cruel separation of ability and virtue; let it be allowed therefore to an individual to repeat it. Had such a daring mind,—had such an invincible courage, had such inexhaustible resources been employed in seeking true glory, and the real interest of mankind, France might have hailed the day which had given to her Napoleon; and Europe, regenerated but not crushed, might have welcomed his salutary purgation. There are times (let no one deny it), when the most ancient governments require a reforming hand, and when the field is only refreshed and fertilized by the fire which devours it rank growth.

June 15th.—This day, at break of day, the army put itself in motion to enter Belgium. The second corps attacked the advanced posts of the Prussians which were opposed to it, and pursued them with vigour to Marchienne au Pont. The cavalry of this corps had occasion to make a charge upon some squares of infantry. It broke through them without much difficulty, and made some hundred prisoners. The Prussians repassed the Sambre, and retired in confusion. The French had in truth a just contempt of the Prussians. The campaign would have had little difficulty if we had had only Prussians to contend with.

The second corps continued its movement upon the route towards Charleroi; the light cavalry of our centre immediately followed, and by successive charges, whenever it met the enemy, repelled them to the opposite bank of the river. We now bore down towards the bridge over the river to Charleroi. Whilst the flanks of all the avenue to it were lined by *tirailleurs*, the Prussians employed themselves at the opposite foot to destroy it, and thus impede our passage. But being pressed by our troops, they succeeded only in effecting a slight injury, and then fled. Our sappers and miners, being brought up, very shortly repaired the mischief which the Prussians had executed; and about noon, their labour being finished, our light cavalry entered Charleroi, and took possession of it

In the meantime, the second corps, having effected its passage lower down the river at Marchienne, advanced upon Gosselies, a large town upon the opposite side of the river, and through which was a road to Brussels. The purpose of this movement was to prevent the Prussians from retiring upon this point, when they should be forced from Charleroi by the attack which was then proceeding. The Prussians, thus forced in front, and anticipated upon our flank, retired upon Fleurus, where they began to occupy themselves in concentrating their army.

Whilst the Prussians were employed in this operation, they had to sustain themselves against the repeated attacks of our divisions, who unceasingly interrupted them whilst taking their position. The presence of Buonaparte so electrified the French troops, that the divisions, as fast as they arrived, threw themselves upon the enemy; and with such irresistible impetuosity, as to bear everything before them. They scarcely discharged a musket, but, bayonet in hand, dashed into the thickest of the enemy's masses.

The squadrons of the body-guard of Napoleon made several charges upon the Prussian infantry; it was in one of these charges, that the General Letort, colonel of the Dragoons of the Guard, received a mortal wound.

The French finally succeeded in driving the enemy from all his positions on the Sambre. Towards night the combat ceased; and Buonaparte, after having left the third corps on its route towards Namur, and the second at Gosselies upon the road to

Brussels, returned to Charleroi as his headquarters. The remainder of the army occupied the surrounding villages.

The results of these several engagements were a thousand prisoners, the passage of the Sambre, and the possession of Charleroi and its magazines. But it was a still more signal advantage that it confirmed the courage of the troops by success. Napoleon availed himself of this success and of its fruits according to his usual system. The prisoners were paraded with the artifice of a procession at a theatre, by the effect of which a few bands, carefully repeated, and systematically reintroduced, appear to be an army. Thus the prisoners were marched in presence of different divisions from the front to the rear. It may be imagined that the air resounded with the cries of *Vive l'Empereur*, and the soldiers believed everything done in this auspicious beginning.

In the beginning of this day, the Prussian army, consisting of four corps, were encamped on the line of the Sambre; they fell back to their points of concentration, Fleurus, Namur, Cincy, and Hannut The principal corps engaged with us was that of General Ziethen. This general was at Fleurus, where he received us bravely. Blücher was made acquainted with these events in the course of the afternoon, and (as was afterwards learned), immediately ordered his other three corps (those at Namur, Cincy and Hannut) to make a forced march to Sombref, about four miles from Fleurus, where he proposed to put himself at the head, and give us immediate battle on the next day.

The French army were now upon the territory of their late subjects the Belgians, who invoked us as their liberators, and who had waited our arrival, as they said, to rise in mass. In fact we fell in with some groups of peasantry at the entrance of some villages who welcomed us with *Vive l'Empereur*, but I cannot flatter myself that they appeared very sincere, or that there was a general sentiment in our favour. In truth, they seemed rather to deprecate us not to pillage them than to express their genuine feelings. But, if such were their purposes, they had little success. Our soldiers gave them acclamation for acclamation, but it was totally a different thing to decline the opportunity of plunder. A free vent therefore was given to the torrent.

As soon as the troops had taken even a momentary position in the vicinity of a village, they rushed like water from a broken dam over all the country beneath; Corn, cattle, bread, meat, even household furniture, linen and clothes disappeared in an instant. The village became a mass of ruins; empty houses; broken doors, and the inhabitants flying into the woods and fields. The adjacent fields, hitherto covered with the promise of a rich harvest, seemed like the straw in a stable trodden under foot; and the fires of the bivouacs, leaving their blackening traces in meadows and corn fields, seemed to mark so many places which had been struck by thunder.

As our troops quitted these wretched villages, the inhabitants, a most miserable spectacle, reappeared; and viewing the ruin and devastation of their property broke forth into intermixed sorrow and imprecations. It was really miserable to see them collecting their broken furniture; and with their children in their hands look woefully at the cornfields trodden underfeet, as if one short hour had destroyed the labours of their life; and reduced them from comfort to extreme poverty.

From the information which we received here, it will not admit a doubt that the Prussians were totally surprised, and that the allies expected nothing so little as our attack at this period; on the other hand, it was a part of their plan to have entered on the French territories a few days after that on which we made the incursion into Belgium. The inhabitants themselves were astonished at our sudden appearance amongst them, whilst they believed us occupied in lining and guarding our fortresses. They spoke very ill of the Prussians, and complained of being very ill treated by them.

But though this first success greatly exhilarated the spirits of the French soldiers, it contained but little which could indicate the fate of the campaign. The enemy's army, attacked by surprise, was certainly; put in a situation of much peril and difficulty. It was even uncertain whether they could accomplish the union and concentration of their several corps. Wellington was so far out-generalled; he was disconcerted by an offensive, movement which he had not foreseen, and he had thus lost, the whole plan of the campaign; he had lost in fact the initiative upon which he calculated, and he would now make his movements upon ground with which he was little acquainted.

Such were (and in some degree with justice) the speculations of the best informed amongst ourselves. Others were elevated to a higher point of extravagance; the most unlimited confidence in the fortune and talents of the Emperor, the annihilation or embarkation of the English, our arrival at the Rhine amidst the acclamations of the Belgians, the treasures of kingdoms poured into our military chest, and nations rising in mass to assist and recruit us, all these were the dreams of the night of the 15th. It seemed as if one kind of temper possessed every one, and that the madness of the Emperor had passed in rapid contagion through every individual of the army.

Upon this very verge of most astonishing events, it is impossible not to reflect, how very near all these extravagant hopes were about to be realized, —how very little was wanting that the Emperor Napoleon had obtained as usual a victory as he actually sustained a defeat. Let the narrators of the campaign, and particularly those who were not present, deceive themselves and flatter their several nations as may suit them; but let me inform them of this tremendous truth,—it was within a very hair that the victory of Waterloo was obtained by the English,—I say the English, for the Prussians were out of the question. They could have effected nothing, if the English had not already done it for them. They (the Prussians), are all made of the same stuff as their king,—when the French nation was exhausted by misfortunes and by previous battles, the King of Prussia and his people had the spirit to attack them. But who such crawling slaves, both prince and people,—who such sneaking flatterers, both prince and people, as His Majesty of Prussia, and these now proud Prussians. Alas, how have the crimes of Napoleon degraded France, when France is given over in punishment to such a race as this—But we here go before our *Narrative*.

June 16th.—On the morning following the above, (June 16th,) the army put itself in march, the Emperor Napoleon, his fortune, and his crimes, at their head.

31

The command of the left wing, composed of the first and second corps of infantry, and of four divisions of cavalry, was given to Marshal Ney, who arrived at the headquarters in Charleroi the preceding evening. He was ordered to proceed by Gosselies and Frasnes upon the highroad to Brussels.

The centre, in which was the third and fourth corps, with the 6th, corps and the Guard in the reserve, was directed upon Fleurus. Marshal Grouchy, with his cavalry and some infantry, manoeuvred towards the village of Sombref upon the road to Namur.

In debouching from Fleurus, we instantly discovered the Prussian army, whose principal masses were drawn up in condensed columns. They were stationed upon the *plateaux* which joins the windmill of Busse. Their position was along a ridge of heights, in the immediate front of which, at the bottom of the hills, was a deep and woody ravine, and which extended in front of their whole line. Its right was *appuyed* on the village of St. Amand; its centre at Ligny; and its left, of which the eye could not perceive the termination, extended itself towards Sombref, and prolonged itself indefinitively upon Gembloux and the route to Namur. All these villages, which were very considerable in themselves, and were strongly situated upon rough and intersected ground (*terrain inegal et intre-coupé*), were in advance of the ravine above mentioned, ,and were well manned with infantry.

Having duly recognized the position (an art in which he excels every man of his age) the Emperor ordered the suitable dispositions to attack it. His mind, his eye, his whole deportment, were now on fire.

The first corps, which made a position of our left, together with two divisions of heavy cavalry, was posted in the rear of the village of Frasnes,—that is to say, a little to the right of the high road to Brussels, so as to be in readiness to move itself to any point in which it might be wanted.

The third corps was directed in columns of attack upon the village of St Amand.

The 4th advanced upon Ligny, having the guard, the 6th corps, and a numerous cavalry in reserve.

Marshal Grouchy, with the divisions on the right, made his advance towards Sombref.

The third corps began the fire in attacking the village of St Amand, where it met with an obstinate resistance. It carried it, however, at the point of the bayonet, but was again charged by the enemy, and compelled to abandon it.

In the meantime, the fourth corps precipitated itself with great alacrity upon Ligny, and a most obstinate conflict was commenced upon this point Each party fought with the utmost desperation, and for a long time there appeared no yielding or thought of yielding upon either side.

In the same moment, our two wings had come to the engagement with the opposite wings of the enemy; our right, directing itself against the enemy at Sombref, whilst our left advanced against Frasnes.

Every part of both armies (our reserve alone excepted) was thus engaged; the affair therefore was now general, and the cannonade, increasing very instant, roared in tremendous horror along the lines.

Upon both sides was the conflict sustained with the same resolute courage,—I had almost said, the same sanguinary obstinacy. I really know not how to describe the inconceivable fury and exasperation of the soldiers on both sides; it seemed as if every man had to avenge himself of some personal injury, and saw in his adversary only his implacable enemy. The French refused to give or take quarter; the Prussians, it is added, had previously announced the intention of massacring all the French who should fall into their hands. The chief fury of the enemy seemed directed towards the Imperial Guard. The French themselves regarded all the Prussians and other Germans as fugitive slaves, and treacherous malefactors. In a word, the mutual hatred was inflamed by the memory of past injuries, and the certainty that whoever should be victors, the victory would be abused by cruelty.

The villages, which were the scene of action, were taken and retaken several times, after the most horrible carnage. Those of St Amand and Ligny were disputed with an invincible desperation. But the French succeeded in establishing themselves in the churchyard of St. Amand, and in maintaining themselves there in despite of the repeated efforts of the Prussians to expel them. The conflict, however, was truly terrible upon this point, and was so doubtful, that Buonaparte sent in all haste to seek the first corps to reinforce the combatants in this quarter. By this movement, the left wing, which was at this moment engaged with the English army at Frasnes, and which had succeeded in repelling the English from the heights of Frasnes to the farm of Quatre Bras, was greatly enfeebled; and what added still to the error of having moved away this important reserve of Marshal Ney, was that Napoleon had not the consideration to inform the marshal of this subtraction of the greater part of his force.

The first corps had moved off, in its new direction upon St Amand, about an hour, when the English army, being considerably reinforced by the Prince of Orange, resumed the offensive, and began to repel with much vigour our *tirailleurs* and advanced columns. On the flank of the high road to Brussels was a wood; the English occupied the verge of it, and were separated from us by a hollow way in the form of a ravine.

But between the wood and the ravine were numerous *plateaux*, which formed advantageous positions for cavalry. Some of them were either in advance of the ravine, or had an easy passage over it. These *plateaux* were suddenly covered with battalions of infantry supported by a formidable cavalry, which confident in their reinforcements, now boldly advanced; and threatened to charge and pierce our opposed line. Our troops, wearied by their previous advantages, seemed to retreat from new efforts. The moment was critical, and it became necessary to call up the reserve. Marshal Ney, however, little alarmed at these appearances, because he reckoned upon his first corps in reserve, now sent it the order to come up, and to charge the enemy. But how great was his astonishment and embarrassment, when he learned that Buonaparte had already marched it off to another point.

He immediately ordered the 8th and the 11th Cuirassiers, who happened to be at hand; to charge the first battalions. This charge was executed with the greatest bravery; but these battalions, being supported from behind with the infantry which filled the wood, were enabled to return such a terrible fire upon us, that our *cuirassiers*, being repelled in their attempt to pierce them, were compelled to make a wheel round; and as always happens in such cases, retired in much disorder. It was in this charge, which, however unfortunate, was executed with the greatest resolution, that a *cuirassier* of the 11th regiment took a colour of the English 34th regiment.

The retrograde movement which was now sensibly beginning, and the multitude of wounded soldiers who threw themselves into the rear, began to excite a manifest terror amongst their comrades. The waggoners, the servants, the attendants of the camp of all kinds, saved themselves with precipitation; and communicating their panic to all they met, soon clogged up the road to Charleroi. The rout indeed in this point (Ney's command) was beginning to be complete; everyone was flying in confusion; and the cry of "the enemy, the enemy" was general.

But the evil was not in fact so great as it appeared, and therefore was repaired. This marshal, the bravest amongst the brave, was not to be daunted or confounded by a slight disaster. General Roussard, with his division of *cuirassiers*, hastened in a long trot into the front of the English, and reassured the fugitives by his presence, and in good part re-established the battle. Our infantry, taking their position upon the heights of Frasnes, were compelled to abandon all purpose of a more forward movement; they confined themselves, therefore, to maintaining this position, and they succeeded in it.

Such was the effect of Napoleon's withdrawing the first corps from Marshal Ney. And the first corps was as useless to the Emperor, as it would have been effectual to Marshal Ney. It was employed only in marching and in returning.

In the meantime the fire continued with increased vivacity along the whole line, and particularly towards Ligny, where the greater part of both armies were assembled, and upon which therefore each directed its main efforts. The cannonade, indeed never relaxed for an instant; and our artillery, as far as I could form a judgement from what I saw, made a most horrible havoc in the Prussian columns, which being posted in masses on the opposite ridge of hills, and upon *plateaux* just below our batteries and position, afforded us a point-blank aim at less than half cannon-shot. On the other hand, our own troops, carefully posted in the sinuosities of the ground, and at the foot of the hills, were comparatively very little exposed to the Prussian artillery; which thus, (like those troops themselves) made more noise than effect, and reminded every military man of the ferocious whiskers and cowardly hearts,—the warlike dress and insignificant minds, of the Prussian Officers.

About seven in the evening, we were masters of the villages, but the Prussians still retained their positions behind the ravines. Buonaparte had all along manoeuvred so as to be enabled to make a sudden movement upon the rear of the ravine; he saw that the occasion was now at hand, and he instantly directed his Imperial Guard and all his reserve upon the village of Ligny.

This bold and most skilful movement had for its object to separate the right of the Prussians from the rest of their army, and thus to intercept it from making a retreat upon Namur.

The guard moved forwards at the *pas de charge*, being supported, moreover, by a numerous cavalry and a most formidable artillery. It forced the village and in despite of a shower of balls cleared the ravine. The Prussians were for a moment daunted, and seemed about to fly; but suddenly resuming their courage, recommenced a tremendous fire upon us whilst in the ravine. A sanguinary content again began, till the Imperial Guard, rushing in front up the ravine, charged the Prussian squares with the bayonet.

The Prussians even yet stood their ground for a time. But at length nothing could resist the impetuosity of the French grenadiers; they forced and cut their way in every direction. The Emperor finished the business at this moment by bringing up the cavalry to charge. The Prussians, thus pierced in every part, and seeing all their courage of no avail, now began their retreat, abandoning to us the field of battle, covered with the dead and wounded, and several dismounted cannon. The Imperial Guard took possession of the ground quitted by the enemy, and the cavalry pursued them.

Whilst this decisive operation was effected at Ligny, the third corps endeavoured to occupy the right wing of the Prussians, with the purpose of masking the previous operation upon Ligny. But the enemy's generals, seeing the purpose of this feint attack, and seeing at the same time the repulse of his left from Ligny, commenced a well disposed retreat, which was now general upon all points of the Prussian army. The enemy now only fought to secure its retreat, which they effected by filing off in columns upon Gembloux and Namur; a strong rear-guard occasionally fronting to repel our attacks.

But as the enemy were defeated, and their columns were soon in the act of flying with more precipitation, we applied ourselves to the pursuit The night, and the fatigues of the soldiers, prevented us from executing this purpose with any effect We were compelled to content ourselves, with passing the ravine, and occupying the ground hitherto possessed by the enemy. At ten, the fire had ceased upon the whole line, and our army was in bivouac.

Our soldiers and officers now recounted in triumph the acts and successes of the day, and as usual we rather exaggerated them in our relations to each other. According to some of my comrades, the whole Prussian army was destroyed, and more than 25,000 killed and wounded of them were left on the field of battle. Others reported, that Marshal Blücher had been killed in the field, and that Marshal Grouchy had just transmitted a dispatch that he had made more prisoners than he knew how to dispose of.

The truth is, that the result of the day was greatly glorious to the courage of the French. Marshal Blücher, having his horse killed whilst in the act of galloping to a charge, fell to the earth, when his horse rolled over him, and happily concealed him. In this state, and the night being dark, he was passed by the French *cuirassiers*, and owed his life only to these circumstances. Upon the part, of the French, no one, I presume, will deny that we completely defeated the Prussians, drove them out of the field, and took possession of their positions. As to the rest, the field of battle was covered with Prussian carcases, and the number of their killed was evidently enormous. But with the exception of the wounded, there were but few prisoners,

Upon the left, where the combat was less ferocious (*acharné*) though still active and incessant, the battle was equal; the English appear to have suffered a very heavy loss, and the two parties remained upon the positions which they occupied in the commencement of the action. I was told of the death of the Duke of Brunswick, and the report of my comrade added, that of General Lord Hill. The Duke of Brunswick was killed by the fire of the division commanded by Jerome Buonaparte; he died bravely at the head of his men, another victim, from this illustrious family, to the wars of Europe. Some of our officers had the littleness of mind to indulge in pleasantries on this incident, but the feelings of every military man will devote them to just contempt.

In a word, the battles of Ligny and Quatre Bras were honourable to the French soldiers and generals, and paved the way to that greater battle which was at hand: a battle in which we ought to have conquered, and should have conquered, had not the hand of providence been against us; that will, which enervates the hand of the mighty, and confounds the counsel of the wise. Hitherto everything was in our favour; the Prussians were beaten, and in another engagement would have been ruined. And the English had only escaped by an error of the Emperor, and the consequent enfeeblement of Marshal Ney in the moment of victory.

One result of this battle was to separate the Prussian and English army entirely from each other, and in a great degree to intercept the communication between them. This advantage was the more valuable and important to us, as it now required only a small and weak corps to observe and pursue the Prussians; and thus it enabled the Emperor to direct his entire strength against the English.

It was with the intention of realizing, this project, that on the 17th, as soon as the day broke, Buonaparte, leaving the third and fourth corps, and the cavalry of General Pajol, under Marshal Grouchy, to observe and pursue the Prussians, directed his own march towards Quatre Bras, taking with him the reserve and the 6th corps.

The English appeared to occupy the same position as the preceding evening. Buonaparte, upon reaching them, employed himself in reconnoitring; and the French army remained in observation and in collecting itself till about eleven in the forenoon,—waiting the arrival of the troops of the right, who were placed in position as fast as they came up. It rained incessantly; and the roads, which the preceding rains had already injured, were now still more impracticable for the artillery.

All the dispositions were now ready for attack; and the French masses having now assembled and united, were in march in line upon the heights of Frasnes, when the Emperor perceived that the Duke of Wellington, by a set of masterly manoeuvres, had succeeded in masking a retreat, in which he had already made a great progress. The Duke had been compelled to this movement by the unexpected result of the battle of Ligny, and having determined upon it, he executed it with that exactness, that compact and wellconnected set of movements, which is characteristic of this celebrated English general; and in which he is excelled by no general living, though he may be equalled by that marshal, and by that marshal alone, whom Europe as well as France proclaims the[1] bravest amongst the brave; that marshal, whose errors are the subject of regret to all honourable and feeling Frenchmen.

The Duke had employed not only a part of the night in effecting this retreat, but even that part of the morning during which we were collecting in front of him. We now beheld his troops upon the hills, upon the entrance of the wood, and as if in position upon the roads; but these troops were nothing but a strong rear guard, destined to support and cover the movements of the main body in front, and which movement the rear followed as soon as it was completely effected. Buonaparte, perceiving this play, as it may be truly called, now applied himself with much alacrity to the pursuit; he put himself at the head of his cavalry, and ordered the army to follow him in quick march

1. Marshal Ney.

towards Brussels.

During this rapid march, the ardour of the troops was incredible; and the soldiers, not understanding the movement of the English so well as the Emperor, saw nothing in it but a precipitate retreat We now promised ourselves that the labour of the war was over; that the English, the main and best hope of the Allies, were on flight to their ships, and that we were in triumphal march upon Brussels. With respect to the Prussians, we never had but one feeling, that of angry contempt; and truly indeed, if the English had been disposed of, we should certainly have whipped these bearded boys, and their savage pedagogue, to Berlin.

In these gallant spirits, and high coloured expectations, we marched with vigour and alacrity towards Brussels; each jesting with each other, and anticipating the amusements of Brussels. The artillery, the equipages, and the infantry of the army, filed along the road, with a degree of precipitancy and encumbrance; whilst the cavalry proceeded along the flanks through meadows and cornfields, which, trampling under their feet, they reduced to dung. The horses sunk to their bellies in the black and soft soil of the fields through which they passed, a circumstance which delayed our progress, and but for the high state of our spirits would have rendered our march painful. But Hope herself preceded us with her most promising flag; we marched under her purple banner, and promised ourselves only certain victory, and a lasting glory.

The Emperor Napoleon, as if summoned onwards by the bright star of his destiny, was at our head; his very horse seemed sensible of his rider; and the army, having so often known his undoubted talents, and still more frequently his most extraordinary fortunes, saw nothing in him but the conqueror of Europe, and the restorer of the French name.

These feelings were redoubled as we perceived the retreat of the enemy from the hills; and in a still more lively and animated manner, when we happened to fall in with some caissons, *voitures*, &c. which the enemy had abandoned on his retreat.

We now passed over the field of battle of Quatre Bras, and

my feelings were much excited by the number of dead and wounded, French and English, whom there had been no time to remove. It was impossible not to recognise how murderous the conflict had been, but there were manifest proofs that the English had suffered more than the French. The ground in front of the wood where they were in position,—the *plateaux* which separated the wood from the road to Brussels, and particularly the hollow way, were actually heaped with carcases, the greater part of which were Scotch, a nation whose gallantry every one must acknowledge, whilst at the same time they must lament their known cruelty.

Their singular costume, a striped plaid, and leggins instead of stockings, arrested our attention; our soldiers seeing that they had no breeches, gave them the ludicrous appellation,—the British *sans culottes*. It is the character of this people (the Scotch) to be the best soldiers and servants in the world; for having no feelings which interfere with obedience to discipline or command, they go strait forwards according to the will of their commander.

The Emperor, with his *avant garde*, continued the pursuit of the English till night, and did not stop his progress till he reached the entrance of the forest of Soignes, where the enemy began to assume a posture, and to make a stand, which required a more regular attack than there was now daylight to execute. After having cannonaded them as long as the light permitted, the Emperor put his troops in position, and established his head-quarters at the farm of Caillou, near Planchenois. The principal masses of the army encamped at Genappe, and in the environs of that small town.

The night was truly horrible. A continued rain, which fell in torrents, caused the troops to suffer most cruelly. Being bivouacked in the midst of meadows and cornfields, which they had trampled under their feet so as to render the soil the consistence of a deep and black mud, our sufferings may be imagined,—no shelter; no dry ground to repose upon, and a sky opening itself to deluge us in torrents. I never remember a night of more cruel suffering, and which indeed well prepared the way for a bloody tomorrow.

We had all only one opinion with respect to the purposes of the English. We persuaded ourselves, that they would employ the night (the night of the 17th) in continuing their retreat None of us doubted but that we should be at Brussels on the next day. In a word, we considered the campaign as already concluded, and that we were now only in chace of a fugitive enemy. Marshal Grouchy, as we believed, was at Namur, and would arrive at Liege on the next day, and about the same time in which Buonaparte would enter Brussels.

These hopes were confirmed by some deserters who were brought in by the sentinels. They reported to us (being in fact nothing but spies for the enemy), that the Belgians were all about to declare for us, and that they waited only for the confusion of a battle to pass over to us in mass. The Duke of Wellington truly was acquainted with their purpose, and with the view of preventing it, had disposed of them in the rear. But that nothing could eventually restrain them from the declaration of their feelings, and from acting in conformity with them, and that the Duke had the greatest difficulty to prevent them from falling upon the Prussians.

Third Day, June 18th.—This day,—so fatal for France, if we must consider our happiness to be in our military success,—this day, fraught with so many vicissitudes, and in which no one would have promised victory to the side to which it was finally given, at length dawned, and the army was at the same time put in battle array, the Emperor in person commanding all the dispositions. Never did he appear a greater commander. Let justice be done to him even by those who promise themselves happier days under another dynasty. It does not become a soldier to speak the language of a courtier.

Our first surprise, as the day broke, was to see that the English had not only not fled,—had not only resumed their position, but seemed moreover resolved to defend it Buonaparte, who had no apprehension during the night, but that they would escape the punishment which he designed for them, was animated with a most sensible joy, at seeing them at their post; he was too fond of the game of war, and thought that he played it too well to have any pleasure in a game only abandoned to him. He could not retain the expression of his feeling to those who were around him.—"Bravo!" said he, "the English!"—"*Ah! Je les tiens donc,—ces Anglois* . . . I have them then,—these English."

Without further circumstance, he now hastened up, with all that imprudent impatience which characterises him, the march of all the columns in the rear; and without any other information than what his eye afforded him, without knowing either the position or the forces of his enemy, without ascertaining that the Prussian army was held in check by Marshal Grouchy, he resolved to attack them on the spot.

The French army, which consisted of four corps of infantry (including the guard) and of three corps of cavalry, formed an effective force (I do not think I underrate it) of 120,000. About ten in the morning of this day (the 18th of June) the whole of this force was assembled in advance of Planchenois. The position was upon two eminences, or short ranges of heights, parallel to two opposite ranges occupied by the English army, the English having taken their position upon some *plateaux* situated in advance of the forest of Soignes, to which forest it was *appuyed*.

Towards the centre of the line, which was upon Mont St. Jean, in the rear of the mount, and around the farm of the same name we perceived some strong and deep masses of infantry; they crowned a vast *plateau* or platform of ground, in the front of which we saw a line of redoubts, the earth of which having been recently dug and heaped, seemed of a different colour from the soil.[2] This *plateau* extended itself on both sides along the edge of the forest, but the line, to appearance at least, diminished in depth as it extended, and was covered with batteries.

The right of the English army was *appuyed* upon the village of Merke Brain, having in front of it the farm of Hougemont, surrounded with intersected ravines or deep descents; their left was extended towards Wavre, and was likewise covered in front

---

2. The following is the note of Walter Scott, in his Poem, *The Field of Waterloo*, upon this statement of the writer of this *Journal*:—"This Narrative, *The Relation or Journal of Three Days of the Battle of Waterloo, by an Eye Witness*, is an incomparable history of this battle, and indeed the only authentic Narrative of all the incidents of this battle. I am much indebted to it, but he errs as to the redoubts, of which there were none."

by a ravine and the farm of La Haye Sainte. We could not follow this line with our eyes through its whole extension; but it appeared to us to terminate behind the village of Smonhen, where was the position of the Brunswick troops.

Generally speaking, with the exception of the great *plateaux* in and about Mont St. Jean, which formed the centre of the English line, we saw but a few troops; but naturally supposed what the event afterwards justified, that they were stationed, and thereby hidden, in the gorges which separated the *plats* from the forest, and in the forest itself.

The headquarters of the Duke of Wellington were at Waterloo in the rear of all his lines; and the lines, as may be seen by the plan which accompanies my journal, were so established as to cross and to cover the roads of Brussels and Nivelles.

Scarcely were the French troops assembled and drawn up in battle array, when the Emperor took his stand upon an elevated scaffolding situated a short distance from where he had slept, upon the right of the road, and near the farm of *La Belle Alliance*. From this station he had the command of the field; and after a momentary reconnoissance, seeing his own troops in due order, he sent the command to begin the fire. He occasionally descending from his scaffold, walked backwards and forwards, his arms crossed upon his breast, at a short distance from his staff, who stood in a group behind him. The weather was stormy; and some showers fell at intervals. This weather continued the whole day.

Our corps was placed on the left, and marched against the farm of Hougemont. The first corps appuyed its left on the high road, and marched against the English centre. The 6th corps formed our right. The cavalry was distributed throughout our line, but the strongest columns of it were in our wings, and particularly in the right wing with the 6th corps. The Imperial Guard was in reserve upon the heights in the rear.

The battle began a short time before midday? The French cannon now opened in tremendous roar: and several bodies of *tirailleurs* advanced to take suitable positions.

The operations of the day were now commenced by our left

making an attack upon the farm of Hougemont The enemy had strengthened their position with great art; they had made loopholes in the walls of the buildings, and thence fired upon us with great advantage. The battle upon this point became gradually most desperate, each side reinforcing its party. Some of our battalions and squadrons, making a detour round the angles of the position, lanced themselves upon the masses in its rear. The enemy, seeing this attack, reinforced their columns, whilst our generals did the same. The conflict was accordingly bloody, desperate, and unyielding.

In a short time afterwards, whilst the conflict on our left and the English right was thus proceeding, our right likewise marched upon their left; they were received by the English with the same steadiness, and a combat of similar desperation accordingly ensued.

The two wings being thus engaged upon both sides, our centre, advancing gradually to correspond with this movement of our wings, marched towards the English centre, so that the whole line on both sides was now engaged.

It was now nearly two o'clock in the afternoon, and we had been engaged about an hour, when the English army, evidently yielding before the impetuous gallantry of the French, was sensibly retreating. The combat had indeed been murderous, and the cannonade and musquetry were but too well served on both sides. Our front lines advanced as the enemy retreated, and our year closed up towards it. The artillery was brought in advance along the whole line.

Our troops were thus gradually all engaged, and were fighting in the midst of the greatest obstacles and difficulties; the soil under our feet having no tenacity, and the surface of it being hilly, abrupt, and intersected with dikes, ravines, and hollows, in the gorges and channels of which we were momentarily opposed by troops whose existence we did not suspect, and who were hidden in them till the moment in which they rose up to meet us. We had to make our way inch by inch. The enemy never yielded a spot till they had exhausted every means of defence. The most inconsiderable hillock, or hollow, was taken and retaken repeat-

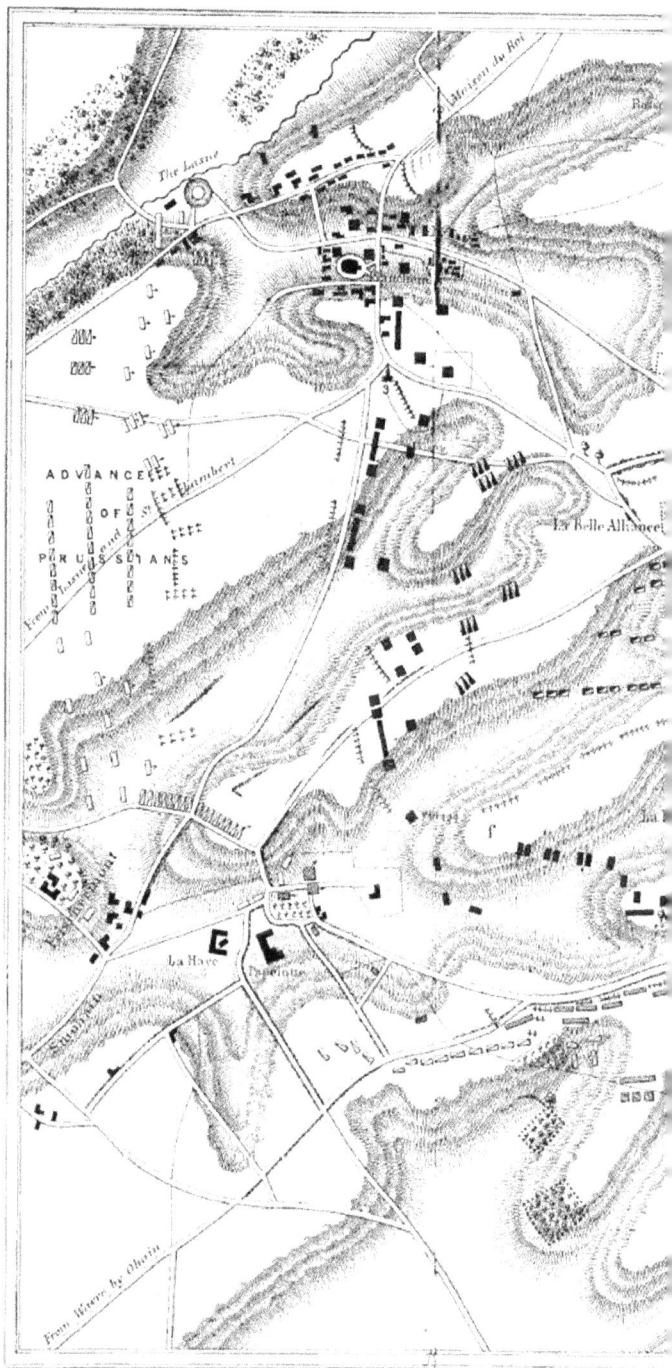

The Lasne

Maison du Roi

Bois

ADVANCE OF PRUSSIANS

St Lambert

La Belle Alliance

La Haye

Papelotte

From Wavre by Ohain

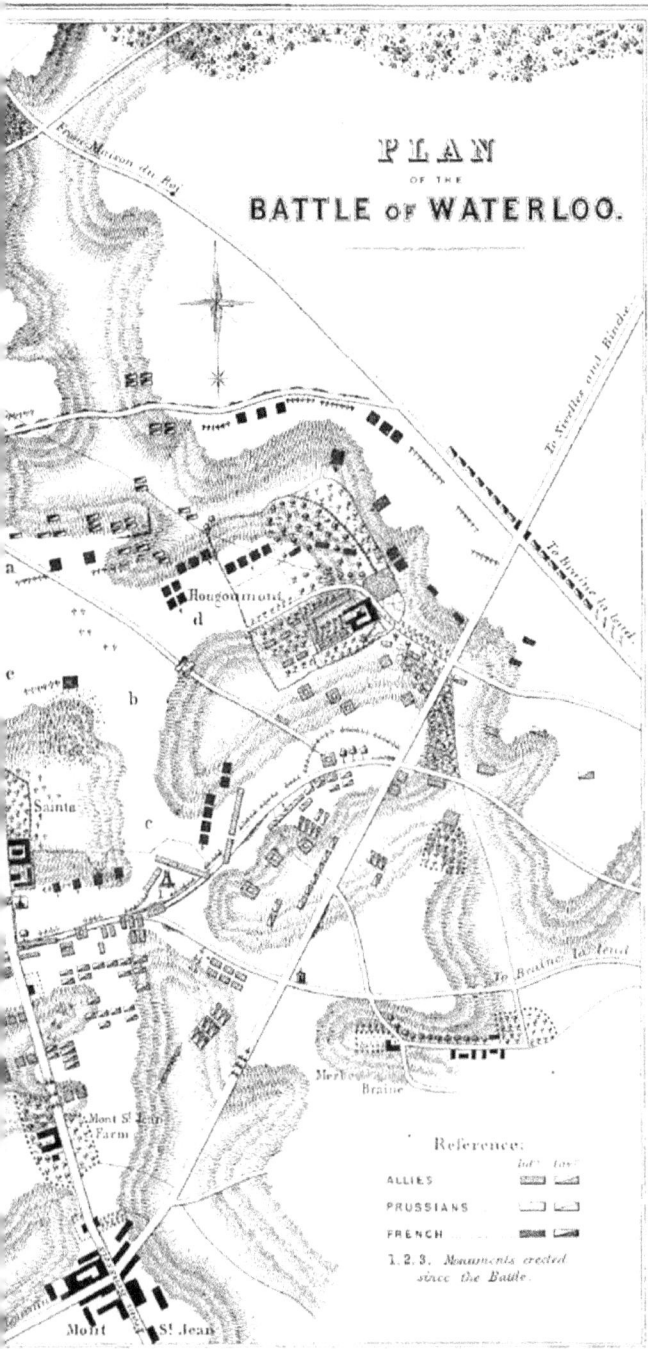

PLAN

OF THE

BATTLE OF WATERLOO.

Route Maison du Roi

To Frettthe and Bierhe

To Bierine Ie Lend

Hougomont

To Braine la Lend

Sainte

Mont St. Jean Farm

Braine

Mont St. Jean

a

d

e

b

c

A

edly. The fire, instead of relaxing, only increased to universality; both sides fought with the most inconceivable gallantry, and the defence was as obstinate as the attack was impetuous.

It was now reported amongst us, that some strong columns were about to make a charge of bayonets upon the position of Mont St. Jean, whilst the cavalry was to make a charge upon some detached points which seemed to be little supported. We expected the result of this great movement, but it was foiled by the obstinate gallantry with which the English defended the farms of Hougemont and La Haye upon their wings. They every moment reinforced their battalions which were posted in these positions; our cavalry, increasing in the same proportion, made successive charges, but the English, like a flux and reflux wave, though one time receding, yet advanced again, and maintained their ground.

Never did I behold a finer spirit of gallantry,—a more resolute and soldier-like steadiness. If for a moment these brave troops (for let them have what is due to them) were pushed from this position, it seemed only by the effect of our superior weight from our superior numbers brought against them; and the moment which restored the equality by the owning up of a reinforcement, restored at the same time the ground they had lost.

The English artillery now made the most frightful havoc in our ranks; we stood in fact point-blank aim for them, and the balls perforated from front to rear through our columns and ranks. Our own artillery answered with the same vivacity, but the enemy were better covered from our fire by means of some eminences which sheltered them. The unbroken thunder of 600 pieces of cannon, all roaring at the same moment, the fire along both lines of at least one hundred thousand musquets, discharged twice or thrice in a minute; the bursting of shells, the blowing up of ammunition waggons,—the hissing of balls, and the groans of the dying, added to the heaps of wounded and killed (the mud being absolutely coagulated with blood), altogether composed a most horrible spectacle; and the more so as the stage upon which so many horrors were acted, was so narrow as to be wholly beneath the eye.

Meantime the French army, in spite of every obstacle, and braving every danger with unshaken coolness and intrepidity, advanced with rapidity. Having carried the points of support of the two wings of the English, it passed the ravine, and reapproaching positions that vomited forth a deluge of balls and of grape shot, the charges which had been commanded were executed without delay, A most formidable first column of attack advanced upon Mont Saint Jean; where the most dreadful firing began.

The French cavalry at the same time threw itself on the eminence to seize on the guns, but was in its turn assailed by the enemy's cavalry, which sprung out in a mass from the windings by which it was concealed. Successive charges were performed, the result of which was nothing but a frightful carnage. The affair was equally sustained, neither side falling back; new columns advanced, the charges were renewed; thrice was the position on the point of being forced, and thrice were the French repulsed, after performing prodigies of valour.

These three assaults, performed without interruption, and with all the distinguishing impetuosity of the French, occasioned the enemy immense loss, and rendered it necessary for him to use the utmost efforts of resistance. Lord Wellington very much exposed his person; and in order to have all his means under his own direction, entered at different times into the hottest of the combat, to shew himself to his soldiers, and to inspire them with confidence by his presence.

The Prince of Orange, whose station was in the left wing, was wounded there at the head of his troops.

Notwithstanding these exertions, the line of the English was within a little of being broken. If we may give credit to witnesses worthy of belief: it is even asserted that the greatest disorder prevailed for a considerable time in their rear, and that they caused their baggage to retreat with precipitation m the direction of Brussels in great confusion, and amidst a general alarm.

However this may be, it is not therefore less certain that they repulsed all our attacks with insurmountable firmness, and that they were able to render them ineffectual, concealing from our observation the disturbance and alarm which attacks so furious, so often obstinately repeated, could not fail to inspire.

At the same time that they began to be agitated with astonishment and terror, the French army was equally struck with hesitation, and the liveliest inquietude. Some dismounted batteries were put in retreat, great numbers of the wounded forsook the columns, and spread the greatest uncertainty for the event of the battle; the acclamation and joyful shouts of soldiers, certain of marching to victory, were followed by a profound silence. All the troops, except the infantry of the guard, were seen in action, and exposed to the most murderous fire; the engagement prolonged itself with the same continued violence, and yet brought forward no result.

The hour of seven was near. Buonaparte, who till now had remained on the eminence where he had placed himself, and from which he had an excellent view of all which occurred, contemplated with a ferocious look the hideous spectacle of so frightful a butchery. The more obstacles increased, the greater appeared his obstinacy. He became impatient of these unforeseen difficulties, and far from fearing to push to extremities an winy whose confidence in him was unbounded, he did not cease to send fresh troops, and to give orders to advance, to charge bayonets, to assault. Several times was it mentioned to him from different quarters, that the affair was unfortunate, that the troops appeared shaken; "Forward, forward," was his reply.

A general caused him to be informed, that he, was unable to maintain his position which was annoyed by a battery; at the same time he inquired what he should do to withdraw himself from its murderous fire, "Seize it," he replied, and turned his back to the *aide-de-camp*.

A wounded English officer, who had been made prisoner, was brought before him. He made various enquiries of him, and amongst others, the force of the English army. The officer told him it was very numerous, and that it had just received a reinforcement of sixty thousand men.

"So much the better," said he, "the more there are, the more we shall beat."

He sent off several of his staff with dispatches, which he dictated to a secretary, and repeated several times in a distracted manner, "Let him not forget to mention everywhere that the victory is mine."

At length the instant was arrived, when, all his attempts having completely failed, it was announced to him, that some Prussian columns were debouching on our right flank, and threatened our rear. He would give no credit to these reports, and answered several times that they had made wrong observations, and that these pretended Prussians were only the corps of Grouchy. He even abused, and sent back in discontent, several of the *aides-de-camp*, who successively came to bring him this intelligence. "Away," said he; "you have been affrighted; approach without fear these debouching columns, and you will be convinced that they are Grouchy's."

After so positive an answer, several of them, in confusion for their mistake, returned with confidence towards the Prussian advanced corps, and notwithstanding the warm fire which these directed against them, approached so near as to run the risk of being taken or killed. It was necessary therefore to yield to evidence, And it was besides impossible any longer to mistake the truth of what was stated, when these columns, filing off as they arrived, made a fierce attack on our right. Part of the sixth corps was sent to support this new shock, in expectation of the arrival of Marshal Grouchy's divisions, which were continually reckoned upon; the report was even spread in the army that they were already in line.

It results from the accounts, that part of Marshal Blücher's army, which after the battle of the 16th had carefully concentrated itself near Wavre, had carefully concealed its march from Marshal Grouchy; and that after being rejoined by the fourth Prussian corps under General Bulow, had with great expedition reapproached the English line to co-operate with the Duke of Wellington.

Marshal Grouchy had in fact pursued the Prussians closely in their retreat upon Wavre, and had in that place attacked the portion of their army which remained there. He was fighting, at the very time that we were also engaged, against some small corps, which he mistook for the whole of the Prussian army, over which he continued to gain signal advantages.

These corps, however, being favoured by the difficulties of a mountainous country, opposed him with a resistance obstinate enough, if not to arrest his march, at least to retard it considerably. They thus succeeded in engaging him at a sufficient distance from the place where the business was really to be decided, and thus presented his having any share in that decision.

For this reason he was of no assistance to us; and thus the English received a considerable reinforcement, whose intervention, which they knew well how to value, and which besides was foreseen, enabled them not only to be fearless of our most vigorous attempts, but to resume against us the offensive, and shortly to overpower us. They therefore reassumed an entire confidence; and calculating their dispositions from the favourable circumstances which presented themselves, they resisted with all their strength, and with an ardour incessantly renewed.

It is besides evident that this operation had been conceited between the two commanders in chief, and that the English defended their position with a steadiness so insuperable, only to give time to the Prussians for effecting this combined movement on which depended the success of the battle, the commencement of which they hourly expected, Buonaparte, who in despite of all appeared to have no doubt concerning the speedy arrival of Marshal Grouchy, and who undoubtedly persuaded himself that he pressed closely on the Prussian army, judged with a determination which nothing could alter, that the moment for deciding the day was arrived. He accordingly formed a fourth column of attack composed almost entirely of the Guard, and after sending off to every point instructions for supporting this movement on which the victory depended, directed it at the *pas de charge* on Mont St Jean.

These veteran warriors attacked the summit with that intrepidity which might be expected from them. The whole army resumed its vigour, and the combat was rekindled along the whole line. The Guard made successive charges, but was in all. repulsed. Beneath the thunders of a dreadful artillery, which seemed to multiply, these invincible grenadiers perceived their ranks to thin under the shots; they closed them with promptness, and with coolness; they continued to march without dismay; nothing withstood them but death or severe wounds; but the hour of defeat was come.

Enormous masses of infantry, supported by an immense cavalry, to which we had none to oppose, ours being totally cut to pieces, fell upon them with fury, and surrounding them on every side, summoned them to yield. They replied, "The Guard does not yield, it dies." No quarter was then allowed; they almost all fell, fighting with desperation, under the edge of the sabres; and the bayonets' points. This frightful massacre was continued while they resisted. But at length, oppressed with forces infinitely superior, and wearied besides with fronting in vain certain death, they abandoned their ranks, and fell back in disorder towards their first position, undoubtedly with the purpose of rallying there.

While things were thus passing near the centre, the Prussian columns, which had arrived at our right, continued to advance, and ardently to press the few troops which were on that point. The loud roaring of the cannon and musquetry was now distinctly heard in the rear of our line, and gradually approached it. Our troops sustained the fight with all their power, but gradually lost ground. At length our right wing sensibly retrograded, and the Prussians, who were turning it, were on the point of debouching on the road, when a rumour was spread, that the Guard had been repulsed, and that its battalions had been dispersed, reduced to a small number, and were retiring in precipitation.

A general alarm spread through the army, its ranks broke in every direction, and sought safety in the most speedy flight. Buonaparte in vain desperately collects for a last effort some battalions of the young and old guard, which had not yet been engaged, and conducts them against the enemy, who had already left his positions in a body. This feeble reserve, intimidated by what was passing around, and likewise overwhelmed by numbers, is speedily overthrown.

The army now, rushing like an overflowing torrent, spontaneously and at the same instant forsook its positions. The artillerymen abandoned their guns, the soldiers of the waggon-train cut the harness of their horses; infantry, cavalry, troops of every description, mingled and confused, now present only a misshapen mass, which nothing can retain, and which flies for its safety toward the road, and across the fields. A crowd of carriages, ranged along the sides of the road in a confused mass, encumber it so as to render it impassable.

Yet the cry of *"sauve qui peut"* had not been raised. This general rout was the effect of an unanimous movement, the causes of which are unknown, and which it would be extremely difficult to assign, if it were not natural to attribute it to the observations which each soldier was able to make within himself of the perilous situation in which we were placed. In truth, the French soldier is never entirely passive, like almost all soldiers of other nations, but he observes, he reasons, and does not in any circumstance obey his commanders so blindly, as to neglect submitting their operations to his own judgement.

No point of direction had been fixed upon, and there was no longer any command which could be heard. The generals and other officers, lost in the crowd which dragged them along with it, were separated from their divisions. Not a single battalion existed, behind which we might rally; and since nothing had been previously thought of to enable us to make a regular retreat, how was it possible to prevent a rout so complete, of which no person had even formed an idea, and which was hitherto unheard of in the French army, already assailed as it had been by so many disasters.

The guard, that immoveable phalanx, which in its heaviest catastrophes had always been the rallying point of the army, and had served as its rampart,—at length this guard, the terror of the enemy, was cut down, and fled dispersed with the multitude.

Each person saved himself at chance,—they drive, they hurry, endeavouring each to precede the one before him; groups, more or less numerous, are formed, and follow passively those at the head. Some are afraid to leave the road, and struggle to obtain a passage through the carriages that cover it; others on the contrary think it dangerous, and leave it to the right or the left, accordingly as reasons well or ill founded influence them. Every danger is exaggerated by terror, and the night, which soon comes upon them, although not very dark, contributes to augment the disorder.

The enemy, perceiving the confused flight of the army, instantly detached a large body of cavalry in pursuit. While some squadrons proceeding along the road fall suddenly on the *ambulances*, which had not time to be prepared for this assault, other formidable columns advance on our flanks. The carriages of the Buonaparte family, seized near the farmhouse in which he had lodged, became almost the first booty of the Prussians, together with a quantity of other baggage. All the cannon which had been formed into batteries, remaining on the ground where they had been used, as well as the caissons which belonged to them, fell at the same time into the enemy's hands. In less than half an hour all the *materiel* had vanished.

The English and Prussians having completely effected their junction, the two commanders, Wellington and Blücher, met at the farm of *La Belle Alliance,* and concerted the means of following up their good fortune. The English had materially suffered in the conflict. Their cavalry in particular, being exhausted with fatigue, would have found it difficult to have followed up the French with sufficient vivacity to prevent their rallying; but the Prussian cavalry being fresh hastened its advance, and pressed closely upon us, without allowing us a moment's relaxation.

The mass of fugitives, being thus urged, rapidly passed over the space of two leagues, which divides Genappe from the field of action, and arrived at that small town, most of them hoping that they should be able to halt there for the night. With the intent of opposing the enemy's progress, they hastened to accumulate carriages in the road, and to barricade the entrance of the principal street.

Some pieces of artillery were formed into a battery, bivouacs were established in the town and its vicinity, and the soldiers dispersed themselves among the houses in search of food and lodging. But scarcely are these dispositions formed, when the enemy appears. A few cannon shot, fired at the cavalry as it came in view, spread a general consternation. The camp instantly breaks up, each individual takes to flight, and the tumultuous retreat is resumed with increased confusion and embarrassment.

During these movements, the fate of Buonaparte was unknown. Some asserted that he had fallen in the combat. When this intelligence was stated to a well known general officer, he replied in the words of Megret, after Charles the twelfth was killed at Frederickstadt, "*Thus ends the tragedy.*" It was stated by others, that after charging several times at the head of his guards, he was dismounted and taken prisoner. The same uncertainty prevailed as to the fate of Marshal Ney, of the Major-General, and of most of the principal generals.

The former, who had under his particular command the first and second corps, had personally directed the different attacks at the centre; and had been constantly in the heat of the battle. It appears that to the very instant when it became certain that it was not Grouchy's corps which was advancing to the right, he had looked forward with hope for the event; but on perceiving that Buonaparte maintained against all evidence that Grouchy was marching into line, and that be caused this, false intelligence to be ostentatiously circulated throughout the ranks, he imputed to him the design of imposing on his troops, and of inspiring them with a confidence prejudicial to their security.

From that moment his views were changed, and he conducted himself with less calmness and confidence. Yet it must be observed, that no aspersions were cast on his conduct in the army, and his courage never was doubted. He only participated in the general uneasiness and discouragement which this circumstance now began to spread. We cannot, however, deny, that from the beginning of the campaign he displayed a profound discontent, which he did not sufficiently dissemble to prevent its attracting the notice of observers. Between him and Buonaparte there existed a misunderstanding, and a species of mutual distrust, difficult to define, but not therefore less apparent.

There is likewise good reason to believe that he entertained some distrust of Marshal Grouchy, which in fact was participated in a more peculiar manner by Buonaparte himself. Such dissentions among the principal commanders must of necessity impede the progress, and disturb the joint effect of all their operations. It was affirmed by a great number, that they had seen Buonaparte without attendants making his escape, in the midst of the crowd, and that they had recognised him perfectly by means of his grey great coat and horse. This last account was the just one. At the moment when the last battalions of the guard which he led were overthrown, driven along with them and surrounded by the enemy on all sides, Buonaparte threw himself into an orchard belonging to the farm of *La Belle Alliance*.

In this place he was met by two officers of the guard, wandering like himself. Having made himself known to them, they conducted him, directing his steps across the parties of Prussians which were scattered over the field, but luckily for him most of them were busied in seizing the carriages and plundering them. Notwithstanding the darkness of the night, he was seen and recognised in many places, where his presence was noticed by the soldiers pointing at him, and saying to each other in a low voice, "*There goes the Emperor, there goes the Emperor.*" These words seemed to him a cry of alarm, and he instantly disappeared with as much speed as the arrangement of the multitude among which he was engaged permitted him. Where were then those loud acclamations which had always attended him, as soon as he appeared among his troops.

The French army continued its disastrous march through the night, scattering its accoutrements along the road, and assaulted every instant with charges by which its disorganisation was rendered complete. The consternation which prevailed in this rout was so great, that large bodies of well armed cavalry and infantry suffered themselves to be made prisoners, without attempting to defend themselves, by a few miserable lancers, whom they might have driven back by merely turning to face them.

At daybreak part of the wretched remains of our army arrived at Charleroi, and part at Marchienne, where they made all haste to cross the Sambre. This unfortunate army, lately so brilliant, now so destitute and harassed with fatigue, presented an appearance which was rendered still more hideous by the great number of wounded who had followed it on foot, or mounted on draught horses. These unfortunate objects, by their paleness, and languor, being covered with the bloody rags, with which they had staunched their wounds, and matching dispersed amidst the confused column which filled the whole breadth of the road, recalled strongly to recollection the scenes of carnage, which were just terminated.

The carriages, as they, approached the Sambre, being retarded in their progress by the passage of those that were foremost, accumulated on the roads leading to the bridges of Charleroi and Marchienne. The enemy's cavalry was not long in making its appearance, and surprised them while thus encumbered. To escape was then the universal object; the affrighted drivers cut asunder their horses' harness, and followed by all who accompanied them, rushed with precipitation towards the bridges, and along the bank of the river in search of a passage. Thus all that remained of the artillery, and of every species of *materiel* was abandoned to the enemy, who likewise took a great number of prisoners.

That part of the army which, having placed the Sambre between themselves and the Prussians, now thought they might halt with safety, after forming bivouacs in the orchards and meadows on the right bank of that river, broke them up with all possible expedition, when it was apprised of the enemy's approach by means of the tumult which his presence occasioned. Without waiting for orders, without attempting to destroy the bridges, and without time for consideration, the disordered flight is again renewed; all set off at once, and each person directs himself as he pleases, not knowing what may be his fate.

At a short distance from Charleroi, they met with two roads, one of which leads to Avesnes, the other to Philippeville. Being uninstructed as to the direction it should pursue, and not perceiving any of its leaders, the army divided itself into two bodies, the largest of which followed the road by which it had come, and proceeded towards Avesnes; the other inclined to the left and marched upon Philippeville. A great number of individuals took refuge in the neighbouring forests, with no other purpose than to avoid the pursuit of the cavalry. Thus the dispersion of the army became every moment more complete, until it almost entirely disappeared.

The last of these roads was that chosen by Buonaparte for his escape. Once more a deserter from his army, he abandoned it without making a single effort to rally it, in the midst of dangers which he seemed to have a satisfaction in rendering still heavier, by giving it up to anarchy and a complete dissolution.

Thousands of soldiers, wandering at hazard, and issuing from the forests in crowds, spread themselves through the country, carrying alarm wherever they came. The wretched inhabitants were thunderstruck on learning, almost as soon as the successes of the French army, its irretrievable defeat, and finding themselves exposed to an enemy rendered more cruel by a victory purchased with his own blood, at the moment when they were filled with joy on perceiving that the theatre of war was proceeding to a distance from them. The fortified places everywhere precipitately closed their gates; and repelling with force the fugitives who presented themselves for admission, obliged them to have recourse to the neighbouring communes, where they committed all kinds of excesses.

In the midst of this terror-struck multitude; Buonaparte, as a fugitive, in greater confusion, and with less confidence than any of them, appeared as a suppliant, requesting to be admitted into Philippeville, The protection of the fortifications of that place was needful to him, to enable him to avoid the active pursuit of the Prussians, who traced him with the greatest vigilance, and had already sent off in this direction numerous parties, with which he was afraid of meeting.

Arrived at the gates of the town, he had to undergo the humiliation of being interrogated by a guard, to whom he represented his rank of emperor, which did not however influence them to allow him to enter, until he was identified by the governor, who was sent for purposely. He was then admitted with a few persons, composing a suite which scarcely exceeded his personal attendants, and the barriers were immediately closed.

A short time afterwards, orders were issued to disperse the collection of soldiers which every moment increased around the city and its entrances. It being rumoured among them that their *illustrious* Emperor was at length found, and that he was in the place, they considered it their duty to encamp around him, flattering themselves likewise that through his protecting care the fortress would at length be opened to them. But Buonaparte's prudence is too well known.

According to his judgement, such a collection of troops might attract the enemy towards this point, and cause his asylum to be discovered; he therefore sent orders to them to continue their route. But having, as an able general, profoundly analysed the means of acting on the *moral* of his troops after a defeat, in order to insure complete and speedy obedience to his command, he adopted a little stratagem, the result of which was certain. A few emissaries, issuing from the town, ran towards the camp in great confusion, crying out, "Save yourselves, here come the *Cossacks*; make haste, here come the *Cossacks*." It may easily be imagined that more was not requisite, and that they all instantly disappeared.

This mob of expelled wretches were the persons who in despairing accents, and overwhelmed with anguish, circulated the lamentable news, that their Emperor was blockaded in Philippeville. This was considered as a positive fact, nor had any person along the roads to Mezieres and Laon the sagacity to conclude that it was nothing more than a well concerted combination, a *ruse de guerre* of quite a new description, invented by the great man to cover the wise march on which his security depended.

Luckily, however, the public mind was not long oppressed by the inauspicious rumour of an event so fatal. Buonaparte left Philippeville after resting some hours there, and proceeded to Mezieres. At the approach of night, he passed by the walls of Rocroi, where it was believed that he would stay. Great part of the inhabitants ascended the ramparts, and he had the pain to hear himself hailed with shouts of *"vive l'Empereur"*, as long as he continued in sight; he appears however to have deemed it more prudent to take advantage of the night in making the best of his way, and therefore made no delay. A few only of the officers who attended him, together with the small number of those of his suite who had survived the disaster, entered the town; two or three horses were all that remained, the carriages of every description having all fallen into the hands of the enemy.

The large body of the army, which had directed its course towards Avesnes and Laon, likewise felt the strongest uneasiness for the fate of Buonaparte; and in this direction, more particularly they were entirely, ignorant of what had befallen him. Convinced that as he was not amongst them he must have sunk on the field of honour, where he had led so many brave men to death, they mourned over the frightful destiny reserved for a person so much valued by them. On learning of his arrival at Paris, in full health and vigour,—eternal disgrace!—how is the indignation to be described, which could not fail to impress their minds.

They had also been deprived of all communication with the right of the army, consisting of the corps of Marshal Grouchy, ever since the battle of Ligny, and although it was expected that they would be met with on the Sambre, no intelligence of them had been received since the defeat. The direction which they had taken was therefore unknown, and the most unfavourable rumours respecting them were circulated.

It was asserted, that not having been timely apprised of the result of the battle of Mont St Jean, the allies had surrounded them in the neighbourhood of Wavre, in the night of the eighteenth and the morning of the nineteenth, and being unable to effect their retreat they were compelled to threw down their arms; and to surrender at discretion, after an obstinate resistance, in which Vandamme was stated to be among the slain. Thus according to these accounts, which although without any absolute foundation appeared extremely probable, the army might be considered as completely annihilated.

Thus was destroyed that fine army, reorganised out of the

many brilliant armies already sacrificed by Buonaparte. That monster seems to have issued from his den, enraged that so many thousands of brave men should have escaped his fury, with the purpose of devouring those who were left. Indeed if we might suppose it to have been his intention to render their destruction complete, there would be no difficulty to discover facts on which to found such supposition, in the measures which he adopted during this short and unfortunate campaign. The enormous faults, of which he was guilty, may however rather be imputed to his want of skill, attended by a temerity without bounds, and to that well known and incorrigible madness, which prompted him on every occasion to push on with blind confidence, without any settled plan of operation, or any calculation of probable occurrences.

The knowledge of the system of warfare which Buonaparte adopted, and never failed to pursue, is what most evidently enabled the generals of the enemy to offer him the bait at which he snatched with so much precipitation, and with such inattention to security. For whatever language the foreign official accounts assume, with the indubitable purpose of magnifying the glory of their generals and the courage of their troops, it is evident that the position of Mont St Jean had been reconnoitred, fixed upon and prepared, as the place to which they purposed to attract the army of Buonaparte, and to be the scene of battle.

In fact, the person who cannot perceive this must be a Buonaparte, one who never was in doubt The evidently calculated retreat of the English on a position so strong; the obstinacy with which they maintained it; the facility of concealing troops and artillery in a vast forest; and, above all, the redoubts and the batteries which they had constructed, would have inspired any other general with a proper distrust, and would at least have given him apprehensions that their fixing themselves there was not the effect of circumstances, but the result of previous intentions.

This suspicion might have been further strengthened by the erection of an observatory of timber, which had been erected on an eminence in front of the forest, from which with good glasses might be seen all that was passing in the plain, as far as the Sambre, and which being without doubt intended to serve as a situation to observe our movements, could not have been erected in a single day.

Under all these suppositions, prudence would surely have suggested an inspection of the ground; and of the dispositions of the enemy. A general of the smallest experience would not have committed such an error as to make an attack without first establishing a communication with his right wing, or at least, without being well informed of the result of its operations. Let it even be supposed that we had succeeded in breaking the English line, which could not have happened without considerable loss.

What great advantage could we have reasonably promised ourselves from it, while they had in their rear a forest which extends fifteen leagues in length and five in breadth? The road which crosses it might be considered as a very narrow defile, in which ten thousand men, with a few pieces of artillery, might with ease oppose the progress of the largest force. Was it therefore necessary to attack in front a position of great natural strength, and was it absolutely impossible to have turned it?

Such are the ideas which would have occurred to a person possessing the smallest skill in the art of war, which the inspection of the ground would of itself have produced in his mind.

Buonaparte however obstinately persisted in perceiving on Mont Saint Jean nothing more than a strong rear-guard, already intimidated, and only assuming a bold aspect to give time to their baggage to file through the forest It was his firm opinion, that to continue the pursuit was all he had to do, and not to fight a battle.

He neither attended to the evidence of his own eyes nor to the observations of some of his generals, who recommended him to suffer the English quietly to evacuate the forest, or at least to defer attacking them, in case they had not effected their evacuation, until the following day. His troops, fatigued with long and heavy marches, and harassed by the continual rain to which they had been exposed all night, were scarcely arrived, when without allowing them a moment's repose, he drove them upon the enemy. Confident that nothing could resist them, he caused them to attack in front an impregnable position; and disdaining to order manoeuvres calculated to render the approach to it less perilous, he yielded them with indifference to the murderous fire of the numerous batteries which were closely planted upon it.

He shortly became impatient of the resistance opposed to him, and always madly aspiring to penetrate and break the enemy's line, he pushes forward all his cavalry, and causes it to perform a desperate charge. In less than an hour it perished by the English cavalry, and was shattered by the volleys of grape shot. In thus sacrificing it, he left himself destitute of the means of pursuing the English, had he been fortunate enough to have defeated them.

Instead of deriving from the immense losses he had sustained a knowledge of the strength and of the designs of the enemy, and instead of pursuing the best measures for avoiding to endanger the safety of the whole army, he comes down in fury from the eminence, whence he had directed his operations, to place himself at the head of his guards; and ceases not to require from them the performance of impossibilities, until overturned and lost in the masses which crush them, they at length may be said to escape from him, and to disappear in the midst of the carnage.

From that moment all was lost, and the destruction of the French army was the more inevitable by being turned at its right, and no precaution taken for retreat. Yet, can it be supposed? Buonaparte alone is insensible of the dangers by which he is threatened. He still wishes to march forward, and collects all his remaining resources to repeat his attempts on the centre. Inconceivable madness! he retains the hope of overturning with a few battalions forces which his whole army had ineffectually attacked.

This is the man who is esteemed the greatest captain of the age! Undoubtedly, and without contradiction he is so, if to gain battles it is only necessary to shed the blood of thousands, by making them rush against each other without a calculation. Yet it cannot be doubted that Buonaparte has shewn at Mont Saint Jean the extent of his capacity; victory was there too much needed by him, that he should not bring into action his full powers. Thus we find ourselves now reduced to the alternative either of allowing that he owes all his victories to chance, or that his intellects had forsaken him during the battle of the eighteenth of June; for his combinations on that day can only be considered as well conceived, by imputing to him the decided intention of causing his army to be assassinated.

Such at least is the judgement formed of them by some generals, whose ability to appreciate them is unquestionable, who even during the contest, being unable to recover from their astonishment, or to repress their indignation, exclaimed aloud, "*Surely this man is beside himself! What will he do? His head is turned.*"

Yet there are some who are of opinion, that setting aside everything relative to the dispositions of the ground, the manner in which he directed the attacks, and the movements which he caused to be executed, bore great resemblance with what occurred at Marengo; so that if suddenly at the precise moment when the victorious English forsook their positions to fall upon us, a formidable column commanded by a Desaix had sprung from the ground, it is highly probable that the affair would have turned in our favour.

If therefore Marshal Grouchy had appeared at this instant, he would in reality have performed the part of Desaix, and it is beyond a doubt that victory would have been ours. But he was at too great a distance from the scene of action to have made so decisive a figure in it. This consideration is a further aggravation of the unaccountable errors of which Buonaparte was guilty at Mont Saint Jean, as he was not by any circumstances compelled to attempt so abruptly an affair of such consequence; and as instead of reducing this right wing to an absolute nullity by neglecting to make good his communications with it, he might without inconvenience have waited until its junction had been effected.

A single day, perhaps a few hours, would have been sufficient for the attainment of this essential object, every probability of success would have been in our favour. Nor in this circumstance can the occurrences which happened be attributed to unforeseen misfortune, since it is evident, that without the possession of any precise information concerning the march of Grouchy's corps, and of the difficulties it encountered, the measures adopted were such as would have been used, had it been ascertained that the whole Prussian army was fully occupied by that corps, or that it was impossible for anything to prevent their co-operation, or to retard their movements. It is acknowledged by all, that when Buonaparte perceived affairs taking an unfavourable turn, he charged at the head of his guards with great courage; that two horses were killed under him, and that he threw himself several times into the midst of the English in search of death.

This act of desperation can only be regarded as afresh instance of madness, and so far from weakening the preposition above of his deficiency of military judgement, on the contrary it corroborates it with fresh proofs. It powerfully contributes to confirm, that incapable of making any provision to secure a retreat, at Mont Saint Jean as on every other occasion, his tactics confined themselves to venturing everything for the sake of breaking through the enemy's line. This will account for the astonishing disasters which have constantly attended his defeats.

It is impossible to avoid lamenting the fate of an army placed at the discretion of a man, possessing an obstinacy so peculiarly invincible, who will not acknowledge any obstacles, and with whom there can be no other alternative than that of conquest or death.

A bravery so inconsiderate in any circumstances is only deserving of serious censure, in a general who owes himself to the safety of his troops. But did Buonaparte really display it? If this question be answered affirmatively, (and it cannot be denied that on innumerable occasions he has braved danger with extreme coolness, and with much temerity), we must as a necessary consequence, recognise in him two beings, essentially different from each other; the one brave, audacious, unreservedly exposing his life in the midst of combats, and fixed on a glorious termination in the field of honour, the other cowardly, pusillanimous, incessantly harassed with the fear of death, and in order to avoid it, braving with effrontery infamy and dishonour.

The latter of these it is, who, so far from making any efforts to rally his army, so far from presenting himself before it to stay its flight, and to preserve its wretched remains, assumes the deserter, and concealing himself in the midst of his soldiers, meanly forsakes them to attend only to his personal safety. If the former has sometimes displayed courage on the field of battle, or has at the least remained firm and unmoved amid those scenes of slaughter with which he so loved to feast his eyes, the other has constantly appeared trembling at the sight of danger, and so frighted with the idea of death, that wherever he found himself dangerously situated, a panic terror has taken possession of his senses, and depriving him of all mental power, has suddenly and irresistibly impelled him to an ignominious flight.

While he thus yielded himself to the impulse of that terror which penetrated him, he stole softly past his soldiers, like a thief who dreads to be recognised by the surrounding multitude. His soldiers, more anxious for his glory than he himself, knew not how more strongly to express the attachment they still bore him, than by wishing that he had remained on the field of battle. "If he had but died!" was their expression.

In vain was he represented to them as a sovereign,—in vain was it attempted to exhibit in full view the distinctions that subsisted between his duties and those of a mere general; in these arguments they would see nothing but a vain pretext to excuse a flight, the infamy of which nothing could extenuate.

However this may be decided, the battle of Mont St. Jean was one of the most sanguinary that have ever happened. The French army, conisting of 120,000 men, after performing prodigies of valour, was almost totally destroyed. Two hundred pieces of artillery, all the caissons and baggage, and a vast number of prisoners fell into the hands of the enemy. Upwards of 20,000 French covered the field of battle with their dead bodies, horribly mangled by the grape-shot. The loss of the English was likewise immense, though less considerable than that of the French, through the advantage of the position they occupied.

The number of slain in the whole army of the Allies is likewise computed at 20,000. Everything concurs to persuade us, that at the commencement of the battle the two armies were nearly equal in number; but the English army was stronger in circumstance, by means of its intrenchments, in which it awaited our attack, and it became considerably more strong, by the effectual co-operation of the Prussians at the moment when the decision was about to take place.

The effects of this battle were easy to foresee, and it was not doubted that the Allies would in a short time be in the French capital. Nothing could afterwards impede their victorious march. The French army, though partly rallied in the vicinity of Laon and Rheims, was too much weakened and discouraged to oppose their progress. They advanced with the utmost rapidity, and in a short time appeared before the walls of Paris, where the only opposition they met with was by the arrival of the corps which formed the right of the French army.

This right wing, which had been given up as lost, had retired with considerable good fortune to Namur, and after marching for eight days in the midst of the Allies, and in a parallel direction with them, contrary to the general expectation, and to all probability, effected its junction with the rest of the army without having suffered any considerable losses.

Seventy thousand men were therefore concentrated before Paris, and threatened to defend that capital. But what was so small a force able to effect against the combined forces of all Europe, now rapidly advancing towards this central point? After a resistance of a few days, highly terrifying to the inhabitants, whose safety was greatly endangered by it, the obstinacy of the troops was overcome. They had resolved on holding out to the last extremity, and conceived themselves entitled to demand the greatest sacrifices. In gradually disposing them to accept a capitulation, and in thus extorting from them their consent to evacuate Paris, France gained in reality a signal victory, the advantages resulting from which are beyond calculation. It is this likewise which in all probability preserved the capital from complete destruction.

The Battle of Mont St. Jean, by occasioning the occupation

of Paris, and the re-establishment of legitimate authority in France, has been the means of terminating the frightful struggle in which Buonaparte had involved us. Undoubtedly the so speedy destruction of so many thousands of men is a most horrible catastrophe; but if on the other hand it be considered as the prompt and unexpected issue of a dreadful war, to the ravages of which all France was about to be given up for an incalculable period of time, there is reason for conviction that it is in reality the least fatal occurrence which could possibly befall us in the melancholy situation to which we were reduced.

In whatever view we examine the state of affairs, supposing even that France were unanimous in her efforts, it is evident, that it was impossible for her to resist the force of all Europe united against her. She must of necessity have fallen after a defence of greater or less length, more or less destructive, but at all events most disastrous to herself. The decisive results of the battle of Mont St Jean have spared her, therefore, if not all the evils, at least great part of the horrors and calamities into which she would have plunged, if she had become the theatre of an active and bloody war.

A prey to the most boundless devastation, she would now have been trampled upon in every sense by numerous armies, who would dispute with each other for her spoils. The country, defended foot by foot, would not have been yielded till covered with dead bodies, and with the ashes of its villages destroyed by fire. The despairing inhabitants would have abandoned their homes to the will of soldiers greedy of plunder, and to whom destruction is insurmountably necessary. In this dreadful supposition, no distinction would have been found between friend and enemy, countryman and foreigner, defender and aggressor; all, equally animated with that spirit of vandalism with which Europe for the last twenty years has been afflicted, would have vied in uniting their efforts to dilapidate, to pillage, and at last totally to destroy our unfortunate country.

Is it not irresistibly proved by facts, that the sacred tie of country is of no avail with men, whom force and violence have placed out of the reach of all laws. If according to the frequent and terrible examples cited by history, the military of every age and nation, whenever they have felt themselves sufficiently strong, have constantly shewn a disposition to form a separate body, and to turn against their fellow citizens those arms which they had confided to them for their defence, what consideration, or what kind of protection could be expected from an army exclusively attached to Buonaparte, and which, in giving up their country to him, had so lately in the face of the world declared themselves his satellites,—the blind instruments of his arbitrary will?

Moreover, this army, inured to a life of wandering, trained in rapine, and governed by the spirit of destruction, was become like the hordes of the Arabs, and owning no country, breathed nothing but war, because war included everything it desired, and restored that unbounded license which constituted the sole object of its wishes. Incapable of the least moderation, and after having ruined every country through which it had passed, France would have been for it only a country still untouched, offering a vast and fertile field for its depredations. This spirit of disorder and unmanageableness which it had borne with it wherever it had appeared, whether victorious or fugitive, had extended itself not only to the foreign troops which had served in its ranks, but also to those against which it had always been opposed.

Our unhappy country could not therefore have escaped those lamentable disasters, which its armies have inflicted on every country which has been successively desolated by their presence, It must however be allowed, that if unfortunately we cannot but acknowledge that the French have set the example of rapine and exaction during their excursions into the neighbouring states, yet have they often been equalled, if not surpassed, by some of the foreign troops; who seem to have made it a point of honour to imitate them in this respect, and there perhaps exists a nation which has really a plea for cruel reprisals, and at the same time might itself be proposed as a model in this respect

But whatever be the motives by which such unworthy abuses of power are excited, how can the reflection escape the perpetrators; that they are only blindly digging a pit into which they must themselves sooner or later fall; for it cannot be dissembled, that it is by these afflicting excesses with which the French armies are reproached, that they have drawn down on their country the reproach of all Europe, and occasioned the dreadful reaction, under the weight of which we at length are labouring. In this point of view, which is rigorously true, they have undoubtedly been more fatal to France than to the very countries which have borne them.

Let us hope, therefore, that this striking example will not entirely lose its effects, and that, for the happiness of all nations, it will enlighten them as to their true interests.

With regard to this general demoralisation, it is evidently the inevitable product of that military system consecrated by Buonaparte, which is unhappily extended throughout all Europe, has taken deep root in it, and (it is to be apprehended) will not be eradicated for a considerable time. Of every principle of morality, and of every rule of religion, he was the unprincipled destroyer, and the declared enemy of the altar. This species of despotism was thus the most severe scourge of empire and of society, or rather neither empire nor society can exist, where it is exclusively established. It gives birth of necessity to continual wars, because interest governs the earth, and man is naturally desirous of power.

Consistently with these maxims, military persons, who are appointed by the laws for the defence of their fellow citizens, and are eminently entitled to respect within their proper functions, are apt to format their duty. Substituting their own individual interest for that of the community, irresistibly governed by the desire of enriching themselves,—of rising to honours and to important offices, they are ready, whenever they possess the means, to convert this public force to their own advantage. Their desires become enlarged in proportion with the facility of satisfying them, and war being their sole means of success, they are of course always ready to incite it

The exclusive preponderance of the military is therefore the heaviest calamity that can afflict a nation, and always draws it into inevitable ruin, Every conquering people has been in its turn conquered. Crushed by the very force of which they had made use, they have been compelled to bend under the iron rod, which, while proud of their conquests, they laid with heavy hand on the conquered. What nation has acquired more of this fatal experience than France.

Who better understands than we the military government for which we have made so many sacrifices, or can more justly appreciate the advantage of conquests, and all the glory of sums. Has not every one of our numerous triumphs cost us a portion of intrinsic strength? And have not all those brilliant armies, full of courage, and acknowledged to be the bravest in the world (and almost constantly fortunate), conducted us from victory to victory to our ruin?

Moreover is it not evident to all, that this wretched system of military despotism causes us to fell back with rapid strides towards the ages of barbarism. Already (as in the times of the anarchy of the Roman republic) have factious legions, acknowledging no laws but their own inclinations, called to reign over the people whom they oppressed the general who had acquired their suffrage; or, as among the Asiatic barbarians, audacious *janissaries* have dared to establish and to dethrone the head of the government at their own pleasure.

We may further observe, that this state of things carries us back to the disastrous period of the establishment of feudal barbarism. Indeed, bow did the feudal system, against which enlightened nations at the present day so unanimously exclaim, become established? Philanthropy is the offspring of civilisation. Men, by nature cruel, and enemies to their fellows, while the ferociousness of their character was unsubdued by education, would of necessity be in a state of war from the earliest periods of their existence, to defend from each other their lives, and the advantages they might possess. It was only by degrees that they united, and that they formed and perfected; gradually and insensibly, the rudiments of that common society in which they now live.

After an undetermined space of time, some portions already

collected (some families perhaps it may be said), formed small tribes, which either attacking or attacked, were for a considerable time in a continual state of mutual hostility. They would therefore choose themselves chiefs, who by the mere effect of that subordination which military service requires, led them without difficulty to servitude. From that period all were soldiers or commanders; each village, or combination of villages, became properly speaking a camp, which moved at the order of its chief.

In times nearer our own, and to speak more particularly of France, after the expulsion of the Romans from Gaul, the respective chieftains of the soldiers who had fought against them settled in different districts with their troops, founding colonies of various magnitudes, which were for a long time governed by military laws; thus forming insulated and independent states, which were enlarged by conquests, or attached to larger states by voluntary submission.

Thus did the most powerful chieftain complete the establishment of his authority. But while the chiefs of smaller tribes acknowledged him as their king or their general, they were not the less tenacious of the right of commanding their own soldiers, who being become their vassals, as they themselves were the *vassal* of another, never took the field but when led by them, and as contingents furnished by them in virtue of their subjection.

It is but a short time since the nobles of Poland armed their dependants according to this mode, and thus restoring them to their original condition as soldiers, placed themselves at the head of them, to assist in a war undertaken or maintained by the sovereigns whom they recognized. The feudal system was therefore founded on the permanent application of military laws to civil institutions.

This despotism went still further; its chiefs, having assumed the supreme station, granted to those who had rendered them particular services, domains peopled with *vassals* reduced to servitude by the laws of war. Conquerors, with the same motives, plundered the inhabitants of the conquered countries, and divided their property among their troops. Thus did Caesar often reward his legions. And what were the dotations which Buonaparte made to his troops but recompenses of a similar description? Were not the towns and villages comprehended in these dotations reduced to a state of *vassalage*, or very nearly?

And if the power of the new proprietors had consolidated itself, would they not have enjoyed all the seignorial privileges which they chose to demand? But was not the same degrading feudality in effect extended over all France; and were not its citizens, who groaned under the yoke of the weightiest oppression, in many respects the *vassals* of that multitude of soldiers, who lived at their cost, devoured all the produce of their property, and the fruits of their labours.

It must therefore be concluded, that military governments are the most oppressive, bear the smallest relation with a civilized and enlightened state of society, and are most adapted for driving us back to the barbarism of the first ages. May the friends of that independence which is worthy of the upright man, and is alone compatible with the maintenance of social order, be persuaded, that servitude originally sprung from the military ranks, and that it has been by gradually removing the yoke of that terrible despotism, that nations have insensibly raised themselves to a more tolerable condition of society.

The combination of every effort against that vandalism which threatens to replunge us into the chaos of barbarism is therefore of the most urgent necessity. It is at length time that order should succeed to anarchy, and that the dominion of force should be superseded by that of the laws.

If Europe have only assumed this military and really terrific attitude, as we cannot reasonably doubt, because she has been reduced to that necessity to repel the unjust and perpetually impending aggressions of France under the direction of the most ambitious and unprincipled of conquerors,—as the cause has now ceased to exist, the reactive effect will of course cease likewise. We have reason therefore to hope, that these late occurrences will restore to every nation the repose which they all demand with equal fervour; and that Europe, instructed by so many calamities and disasters, will quickly lay aside this warlike position, the permanence of which must inevitably give cause for new revolutions.

It is not France that has been vanquished in the lately terminated struggle. She, on the contrary, formed an integral part of the coalition against her oppressor. She is not therefore subdued, but delivered, and cannot under any pretext be treated as a conquered country. The whole country, having rallied around its legitimate monarch, of whom force alone, had deprived it, again finds itself at peace with all Europe. She has therefore a right to demand the enjoyment of the advantages of the peace, to the conquest of which she contributed her share.

She consequently requires of her allies the performance of the solemn promises by which they have bound themselves to her, and which they cannot violate without renouncing the noble title they have acquired of her liberators, and without declaring themselves her implacable enemies. Europe would then be again plunged into an abyss of evils; France, exhausted, would rise in one mass to shake off the hateful yoke attempted to be imposed, the humiliation of which she could not suffer, and torrents of blood would again flow,

But we are enabled to rely too well on the moderation, the prudence and justice, which presided over the councils of the combined sovereigns, and they are too earnestly engaged in promoting the happiness and tranquillity of their own dominions, to give reasonable grounds for fearing an exposure to such horrors.

France, on her part, can in her present situation offer guarantees for the preservation of peace, completely satisfactory, the principal of which is doubtless the character of her sovereign, eminent for his good faith, justice, superior understanding, and philanthropic disposition. It will be his eneavour totally to dissipate that mental intoxication, which unfolding itself in the midst of revolutions, has perverted the present generation, and given it an irresistible bias for disorder and immorality.

It is reserved to the virtue and wisdom, which characterises this pacific sovereign, to give a new impulse to the French character, or rather to restore to it its original state, and to reconstruct on solid foundations the edifice of a liberal, but just and firm government, equally protecting all citizens; zealous for the preservation of public morals, and those institutions which insure the happiness and tranquillity of nations, and to say all in a word, which contains in itself the principles of its duration.

Let those of our warriors who are sincere lovers of their country be convinced, that peace is the only benefit which it requires. May they, like the noble Regulus, whose conduct so justly excites our admiration, now hang up their swords as glorious trophies in commemoration of their achievements, and not take them down until their country shall call on them in its defence. Yielding themselves to agriculture, and the useful arts, which form the happiness and glory of human nature, let them return as peaceable citizens into the bosom of their families.

May they become respectable members of the commonwealth, which will derive honour and riches from their industry, by which they will acquire honour and wealth for themselves; and may they in their turn, becoming particularly interested in respecting the social bond, be the first to dread the disasters of war, add contribute with all their power to avert that terrible scourge, the calamities of which they will be able most justly to appreciate.

Appendix.

SIX OFFICIAL REPORTS OF THE BATTLE OF WATERLOO.

1 PRUSSIAN ACCOUNT.

MARSHAL BLÜCHER'S OFFICIAL REPORT OF THE OPERATIONS OF THE PRUSSIAN ARMY ON THE LOWER RHINE, JUNE, 1815.

It was on the 15th of this month that Napoleon, after having collected, on the 14th, five corps of his army, and the several corps of the guard, between Maubeuge and Beaumont,, commenced hostilities. The points of concentration of the four Prussian corps, were Fleurus, Namur, Cincy, and Hannut; the situation of which made it possible to unite the army, in one of these points, in 34 hours.

On the 15th, Napoleon advanced by Thuin, upon the two banks of the Sambre, against Charleroi. General Ziethen had collected the first corps near Fleurus, and had on that day a very warm action with the enemy, who after having taken Charleroi, directed his march upon Fleurus. General Ziethen maintained himself in his position near that place.

Field Marshal Blücher intending to fight a great battle with the enemy, as soon as possible, the three other corps of the Prussian army were consequently directed upon Sombref, a league and a half from Fleurus, where the 2nd and 3rd were to arrive on the 15th, and the 4th corps on the 16th.

Lord Wellington had united his army between Ath and Nivelles, which enabled him to assist Field Marshal Blücher, in case the battle should be fought on the 15th.

June 16th.—Battle of Ligny.—The Prussian army was posted

on the heights between Brie and Sombref, and beyond the last place, and occupied with a large force the village of St. Amend and Ligny, situate in its front. Meantime, only three corps of the army had joined; the fourth, which was stationed between Liege and Hannut, had been delayed in its march by several circumstances, and was not yet come up. Nevertheless, Field Marshal Blücher resolved to give battle; Lord Wellington having already put in motion, to support him, a strong division of his army, as well as his whole reserve, stationed in the environs of Brussels, and the 4th corps of the Prussian army being also on the point of arriving.

The battle began at three o'clock in the afternoon. The enemy brought up about 130,000 men. The Prussian army was 80,000 strong. The village of St. Amand was the first attacked by the enemy, who carried it, after a vigorous resistance.

He then directed his efforts against Ligny. It is a large village, solidly built, situate on a rivulet of the same name. It was there that a contest began which may be considered as one of the most obstinate recorded in history. Villages have often been taken, and retaken; but here the combat continued for five hours in the villages themselves, and the movements forwards or backwards were confined to a very narrow space. On both sides fresh troops continually came up. Each army had, behind the part of the village which it occupied, great masses of infantry, which maintained the combat, and were continually renewed by the reinforcements which they received from their rear, as well as from the heights on the right and left.

About two hundred cannon were directed from both sides of the village, which was on fire, in several places at once. From time to time the combat extended through the whole line, the enemy having also directed numerous troops against the third corps; however, the main contest was near Ligny. Things seemed to take a favourable turn for the Prussian troops, a part of the village of St. Amand having been retaken by a battalion commanded by the Field Marshal in person, in consequence of which advantage we had regained a height, which had been abandoned after the loss of St. Amand. Nevertheless, the battle continued about Ligny with the same fury

The issue seemed to depend on the arrival of the English troops, or on those of the fourth corps of the Prussian army; in fact, the arrival of this last division would have afforded the Field Marshal the means of making, immediately, with the right wing, an attack, from which great success might be expected: but news arrived that the English division, destined to support us, was violently attacked by a corps of the French army, and that it was with great difficulty it had maintained itself in its position at Quatre Bras.

The fourth corps of the army did not appear, so that we were forced to maintain, alone, the contest with an army greatly superior in numbers, The evening was already much advanced, and the combat about Ligny continued with the same fury, and the same equality of success; we invoked, but in vain, the arrival of those succours which were so necessary; the danger became every day more urgent; all the divisions were engaged, or had already been so, and there was not any corps at hand able to support them.

Suddenly, a division of the enemy's infantry, which, by favour of the night, had made a circuit round the village without being observed, at the same time that some regiments of *cuirassiers* had forced the passage on the other side, took, in the rear, the main body of our army, which was posted behind the houses. This surprise, on the part of the enemy, was decisive, especially at the moment when our cavalry, also posted on a height behind the village, was repulsed by the enemy's cavalry in repeated attacks.

Our infantry, posted behind Ligny, though forced to retreat, did not suffer itself to be discouraged, either by being surprised by the enemy in the darkness, a circumstance which exaggerates in the mind of man the dangers to which he finds himself exposed, or, by the idea of seeing itself surrounded on all sides. Formed in masses, it coolly repulsed all the attacks of the cavalry, and retreated in good order upon the heights, whence it continued its retrograde movement upon Tilly.

In consequence of the sudden irruption of the enemy's cavalry, several of our cannons, in their precipitate retreat, had taken directions which led them to defiles, in which they necessarily fell into disorder: in this manner 15 pieces fell into the hands of the enemy.

At the distance of a quarter of a league from the field of battle, the army formed again. The enemy did not venture to pursue it. The village of Brie remained in our possession during the night, as well as Sombref, where General Thielman had fought with the third corps, and whence he, at daybreak, slowly began to retreat towards Gembloux, where the fourth corps, under General Bulow, had at length arrived during the night. The first and second corps proceeded in the morning behind the defile of Mount St Guibert.

Our loss in killed and wounded was great; the enemy, however, took from us no prisoners, except a part of our wounded. The battle was lost, but not our honour. Our soldiers had fought with a bravery which equalled every expectation; their fortitude remained unshaken, because everyone retained his confidence in his own strength. On this day, Field Marshal Blücher had encountered the greatest dangers. A charge of cavalry, led on by himself, had failed. While that of the enemy was vigorously puling, a musket-shot struck the Field Marshal's horse: the animal, far from being stopped in his career by this wound, began to gallop more furiously, till he dropped down dead. The Field Marshal stunned by the violent fall, lay entangled under the horse.

The enemy's *cuirassiers*, following up their advantage, advanced: our last horseman had already passed by the Field Marshal, an adjutant alone remained with him, and resolved to share his fate. The danger was great, but Heaven watched over him. The enemy, pursuing their charge, passed rapidly by the Field Marshal without seeing him: the next moment, a second charge, of our cavalry having repulsed them, they again passed by him with the same precipitation, not perceiving him, any more than they had done the first time. Then, but not without difficulty, the Field Marshal was disengaged from under the dead horse, and he immediately mounted a dragoon horse.

On the 17th, in the evening, the Prussian army concentrated itself in the environs of Wavre. Napoleon put himself in motion against Lord Wellington upon the great road leading from Charleroi to Brussels. An English division maintained, on the same day, near Quatre Bras, a very severe contest with the enemy. Lord Wellington had taken a position on the road to Brussels, having his right wing leaning upon Braine-la-Leud, the centre near Mont St, Jean, and the left wing against La Haye Sainte, Lord Wellington wrote to the Field Marshal, that he was resolved to accept the battle in this position, if the Field Marshal would support him with two corps of his army.

The Field Marshal promised to come with his whole army; he even proposed, in case Napoleon should not attack, that the Allies themselves, with their whole united force, should attack him the next day. This may serve to show how little the battle of the 16th had disorganised the Prussian army, or weakened its moral strength. Thus ended the day of the 17th.

Battle of the 18th.—At break of day the Prussian army again began to move. The 4th and 2nd corps marched by St Lambert, where they were to take a position, covered by the forest, near Frichemont, to take the enemy in the rear, when the moment should appear favourable. The first corps was to operate by Ohain, on the right flank of the enemy The third corps was to follow slowly, in order to afford succour in case of need. The battle began about 10 o'clock in the morning.

The English army occupied the heights of Mont St. Jean; that of the French was on the heights before Planchenoit: the former was about 80,000 strong; the enemy had above 130,000. In a short time, the battle became general along the whole line. It seems that Napoleon had the design to throw the left wing upon the centre, and thus to effect the separation of the English army from the Prussian, which he believed to be retreating upon Maestricht.

For this purpose, he had placed the greatest part of his reserve in the centre, against his right wing, and upon this point he attacked with fury. The English army fought with a valour which it is impossible to surpass. The repeated charges of the Old Guard were baffled by the intrepidity of the Scottish regiments; and at every charge the French cavalry was overthrown by the

English cavalry. But the superiority of the enemy in numbers was too great; Napoleon continually brought forward considerable masses, and, with whatever firmness the English troops maintained themselves in their position, it was not possible but that such heroic exertions must have a limit.

It was half-past four o'clock. The excessive difficulties of the passage by the defile of St Lambert, had considerably retarded the march of the Prussian columns, so that only two brigades of the fourth corps had arrived at the covered position which was assigned to them. The decisive moment was come: there was not an instant to be lost. The generals did not suffer it to escape. They resolved immediately to begin the attack with the troops which they had at hand. General Bulow, therefore, with two brigades and a corps of cavalry, advanced rapidly upon the rear of the enemy's right wing. The enemy did not lose his presence of mind; he instantly turned his reserve against us, and a murderous conflict began on that side.

The combat remained long uncertain, while the battle with the English army still continued with the same violence,

Towards six o'clock in the evening, we received the news that General Thielman, with the third corps, was attacked near Wavre by a very considerable corps of the enemy, and that they were already disputing the possession of the town. The Field Marshal, however, did not suffer himself to be disturbed by this news; it was on the spot where he was, and nowhere else, that the affair was to be decided. A conflict continually supported by the same obstinacy, and kept up by fresh troops could alone ensure the victory, and if it were obtained here, any reverse sustained near Wavre was of little consequence.

The columns, therefore, continued their movements. It was half an hour past seven, and the issue of the battle was still uncertain. The whole of the 4th corps, and a part of the 2nd, under General Pirch had successively come up. The French troops fought with desperate fury: however, some uncertainty was perceived in their movements, and it was observed that some pieces of cannon were retreating. At this moment, the first columns of the corps of General Ziethen arrived on the points of attack, near the village of Smonhen, on the enemy's right flank, and instantly charged.

This moment decided the defeat of the enemy. His right wing was broken in three places; he abandoned his positions. Our troops rushed forward at the *pas de charge*, and attacked him on all sides, while, at the same time, the whole English line advanced.

Circumstances were extremely favourable to the attack formed by the Prussian army; the ground rose in an amphitheatre, so that our artillery could freely open its fire, from the summit of a great many heights which rose gradually above each other, and in the intervals of which the troops descended into the plain, formed into brigades, and in the greatest order; while fresh corps continually unfolded themselves, issuing from the forest on the height behind us. The enemy, however, still preserved means to retreat, till the village of Planchenoit which he had on his rear, and which was defended by the guard, was, after several bloody attacks, carried by storm.

From that time the retreat became a rout, which soon spread through the whole French army, which, in its dreadful confusion, hurrying away everything that attempted to stop it, soon assumed the appearance of the flight of an army of barbarians. It was half-past nine. The Field Marshal assembled all the superior officers, and gave orders to send the last horse and the last man in pursuit of the enemy. The van of the army accelerated its march. The French being pursued without intermission were absolutely disorganised. The causeway presented the appearance of an immense shipwreck; it was covered with an innumerable quantity of cannon, *caissons*, carriages, baggage, arms, and wrecks of every kind.

Those of the enemy who had attempted to repose for a time, and had not expected to be so quickly pursued, were driven from more than nine bivouacs. In some villages they attempted to maintain themselves: but as soon as they beard the beating of our drums, or the sound of the trumpet, they either fled or threw themselves into the houses, where they were cut down and made prisoners. It was moonlight, which greatly favoured the pursuit, for the whole march was but a continued chace, either in the cornfields or the houses.

At Genappe, the enemy had entrenched himself with cannon and overturned carriages: at our approach, we suddenly heard in the town a great noise and a motion of carriages; at the entrance we were exposed to a brisk fire of musketry; we replied by some cannon shot, followed by a hurrah, and, an instant after, the town was ours. It was here that, among many other equipages, the carriage of Napoleon was taken; he had just left it to mount on horseback, and, in his hurry, had forgotten in it his sword and hat. Thus the affairs continued till break of day. About 40,000 men, in the most complete disorder, the remains of the whole army, have saved themselves, retreating through Charleroi, partly without arms, and carrying with them only 27 pieces of their numerous artillery.

The enemy, in his flight, had passed all his fortresses, the only defence of his frontiers, which are now passed by our armies.

At three o'clock, Napoleon had dispatched, from the field of battle, a courier to Paris, with the news that victory was no longer doubtful; a few hours after, he had no longer any army left. We have not yet any exact account of the enemy's loss; it is enough to know, that two-thirds of the whole were killed, wounded, or taken prisoners; among the latter are Generals Mouton, Duhesme, and Compans. Up to this time about 300 cannon, and above 400 *caissons*, are in our hands.

Few victories have been so complete; and there is certainly no example that an army, two days after losing a battle, engaged in such an action, and so gloriously maintained it. Honour be to troops capable of so much firmness, and valour! In the middle of the position occupied by the French army, and exactly upon the height, is a farm, called *La Belle Alliance*. The march of all the Prussian columns was directed towards this farm, which was visible from every side.

It was there that Napoleon was during the battle; it was thence that he gave his orders; that he flattered himself with the hopes of victory; and it was there that his ruin was decided. There, too, it was, that by a happy chance, Field Marshal Blücher and Lord Wellington met in the dark, and mutually saluted each other as victors.

In commemoration of the alliance which now subsists between the English and Prussian nation, of the union of the two armies, and their reciprocal confidence, the Field Marshal desired, that this battle should bear the name of *La Belle Alliance.*

By order of Field Marshal Blücher,

General Gneisenau.

Brave Officers and Soldiers of the Army of the Lower Rhine—

You have had to struggle with privations, but you have borne them with fortitude. Immoveable in adverse fortunes after the loss of a bloody battle, you marched with firmness to fight another, relying on the God of battles, and full of confidence in your commanders, as well as of perseverance in your efforts against presumptuous and perjured enemies, intoxicated with victory.

It was with these sentiments you marched to support the brave English, who were maintaining the most arduous content with unparalleled, firmness.

But the hour which was to decide this great struggle has struck, and has shewn who was to give the law, whether an adventurer, or Governments who are friends of order. Destiny was still undecided, when you appeared issuing from the, forest which concealed you from the enemy, to attack his rear with that coolness, that firmness, that confidence, which characterises experienced soldiers, resolved to revenge the reverses they had experienced two days before.

There, rapid as lightning, you penetrated his already shaken columns. Nothing could stop you in the career of victory. The enemy in his despair turned his artillery upon you;

85

but you poured death into his ranks, and your progress caused in them disorder, dispersion, and, at last, a complete route. He found himself obliged to abandon to you several hundreds of cannon; and his army is dissolved.

A few days will suffice to annihilate these perjured legions, who were coming to consummate the slavery and the spoliation of the universe.

All great commanders have regarded it as impossible immediately to renew the combat with a beaten army, you have proved that resolute warriors may be vanquished, but that their valour is not shaken.

Receive then, my thanks, incomparable soldiers—objects of all my esteem. You have acquired a great reputation. The annals of Europe will eternize your triumphs. It is on you, immoveable columns of the Prussian monarchy, that the destinies of the King, and his august house, will forever repose.

2. SPANISH ACCOUNT.

General Miguel Alava, in quality of Minister Plenipotentiary to the King of the Netherlands, from the King of Spain, having shared the dangers of the battle, by the side of the Duke of Wellington, addressed his court, dated June 20th, from Brussels, giving an account of the battles of Quatre Bras, and Waterloo, the principal details of which being already given, we think it sufficient to make such extracts as may assist our other information, and to convey an adequate idea of the glory achieved by the unprecedented exertions of officers and men.

Speaking of the battle of the 16th, the general says—

The English guards, various regiments, and the Scottish brigade, covered themselves with glory on this day; and Lord Wellington told me, on the following day, that he had never seen his troops behave better, in all the many years he had commanded them. The French *cuirassiers* suffered greatly on this occasion, for, confiding in their *cuirasses*, they approached so near the English squares, that they succeeded in cutting down with their swords some officers of the 52nd: but that brave regiment, without being appalled, kept up so well supported a fire, that the ground was strewed with the *cuirassiers* and their horses.

Of the battle of Waterloo, General Alava writes as follows:—

I joined the army on the morning of the 18th, though I had received no orders to that effect, because I believed that I should thus best serve His Majesty, and at the same time fulfil your Excellency's directions; and this determination has afforded me the satisfaction of having been present at the most important battle that has been fought for many centuries, in its consequences, its duration, and the talents of the chiefs on both sides, and because the peace of the world, and the future security of all Europe, may be said to have depended on its result.

The position occupied by his Lordship was very good; but towards the centre it had various weak points, which required good troops to guard them, and much science and skill on the part of the general in chief. These qualifications were, however, to be found in abundance in the British troops and their illustrious commander, and it may be asserted, without offence to any one, to them both belongs the chief part of all the glory of this memorable day.

On the right of the position, and a little in advance, was. a country house, the importance of which Lord Wellington quickly perceived, because without it the position could not be attacked on that side, and it might therefore be considered as its key. The Duke confided this important point to three companies of the English guards, under the command of Lord Saltoun, and laboured during the night of the 17th in fortifying it as well as possible, lining its garden, and wood which served as its park, with Nassau troops as sharp-shooters.

At half past ten, a movement was observed in the enemy's line, and many officers were seen coming and going to a particular point, where there was a very considerable corps of infantry, which we afterwards understood to be the Imperial Guard; here was Buonaparte in person, and from this point issued all the orders. In the meantime the enemy's masses were forming, and everything announced the approaching combat, which began at half past seven, the enemy attacking with one of his corps, and, with his usual shouts, the country house on the right.

The Nassau troops found it necessary to abandon their post; but the enemy met such resistance in the house, that though they surrounded it on three sides, and attacked it most desperately, they were compelled to desist from their enterprise, leaving a good number of killed and wounded on the spot. Lord Wellington sent fresh English troops, who recovered the wood and garden, and the combat ceased for the present on this side.

The enemy then opened a horrible fire of artillery from more than 200 pieces, under cover of which Buonaparte made a general attack from the centre to the right with infantry and cavalry, in such numbers, that it required all the skill of his Lordship to post his troops, and all the good qualities of the latter, to resist the attack.

General Picton, who was with his division on the road from Brussels to Charleroi, advanced with the bayonet to receive them; but was unfortunately killed at the moment when the enemy, appalled by the attitude of this division, fired, and then fled.

The English Life Guards then charged with the greatest vigour, and the 49th and 105th French regiments lost their eagles in this charge, together with from 2,000 to 3,000 prisoners. A column of cavalry, at whose head were the *cuirassiers*, advanced to charge the Life Guards, and thus save their infantry, but the Guards received them with the greatest valour, and the most sanguinary cavalry fight, perhaps, ever witnessed, was the consequence.

The French *cuirassiers* were completely beaten, in spite of their *cuirasses*, by troops who had nothing of the sort, and lost one of their eagles in this conflict, which was taken by the heavy English cavalry called the *Royals*

General Alava next mentions the approach of the Prussian army, "which," he observes:

. . . . . was the more necessary, from the superior numbers of the enemy's army, and from the dreadful loss we had sustained in this unequal combat, from eleven in the morning till five in the afternoon.

Buonaparte, who did not believe the Prussians to be so near, and who reckoned upon destroying Lord Wellington before their arrival, perceived that he had fruitlessly lost more than five hours, and that in the critical position in which he was then placed, there remained no other resource but that of desperately attacking the weak part of the English position, and thus, if possible, beating the Duke before his right was turned, and attacked by the Prussians.

Henceforward, therefore, the whole was a repetition of attacks by cavalry and infantry, supported by more than 300 pieces of artillery, which unfortunately, made horrible ravages in our line, and killed and wounded officers, artillerists, and horses, in the weakest part of the position.

The enemy, aware of this destruction, made a charge with the whole cavalry of his guard, which took some pieces of cannon that, could not be withdrawn; but the Duke, who was at this point, charged them with three battalions of English and three of Brunswickers, and compelled them in a moment to abandon the artillery, though we were unable to withdraw them for want of horses; nor did they dare to advance to recover them.

At last, about seven in the evening, Buonaparte made a last effort, and putting himself at the head of his guards, attacked the above point of the English position with such vigour, that he drove back the Brunswickers who occupied part of it, and, for a moment, the victory was undecided, and even more than doubtful.

The Duke, who felt that the moment was most critical, spoke to the Brunswick troops with that ascendency which every great man possesses, made them return to the charge, and, putting himself at their head, again restored the combat, exposing himself to every kind of personal danger.

Fortunately, at this moment, we perceived the fire of Marshal Blücher, attacking the enemy's right with his usual impetuosity; and the moment of decisive attack being come, the Duke put himself at the head of the English Foot Guards, spoke a few words to them, which were, replied to by a general hurrah, and his Grace himself guiding them forward with his hat, they marched at the point of the bayonet, to come to close action with the Imperial Guard. But the latter began a retreat, which was soon. converted into flight, and the most complete rout ever exhibited by soldiers. The famous rout at Vittoria was not even comparable to it

The gallant general then adds several reflections on the importance of the victory; and, in enumerating the loan sustained, says:—

Of those who were by the Duke of Wellington, only he and myself remained untouched in our persons and horses. The rest were all either killed, wounded, or lost one or more horses. The Duke was unable to refrain from tears on witnessing the death of so many brave and honourable men, and the loss of so many friends and faithful companions, and which can alone be compensated by the importance of the victory.

3. BUONAPARTE'S ACCOUNT.

FRENCH OFFICIAL DETAIL OF THE BATTLES WITH THE PRUSSIANS AND ENGLISH.

Battle of Ligny-under-Fleurus, Paris, June 21.—On the morning of the 16th the army occupied the following position:—

The left wing, commanded by the Marshal Duke of Elchingen, and consisting of the 1st and 2nd corps of infantry, and the

2nd of cavalry, occupied the positions of Frasnes.

The left wing, commanded by Marshal Grouchy, and composed of the 3rd and 4th corps of infantry, and the 3rd corps of cavalry, occupied the heights in rear of Fleurus.

The Emperor's headquarters were at Charleroi, where were the Imperial Guard and the 6th corps.

The left wing had orders to march upon Quatre Bras, and the right upon Sombref. The Emperor advanced to Fleurus with his reserve,

The columns of Marshal Grouchy being in march, perceived, after having passed Fleurus, the enemy's army, commanded by Field Marshal Blücher, occupying with its left the heights of the mill of Bussy, the village of Sombref, and extending its cavalry a great way forward on the road to Namur; its right was at St. Amand, and occupied that large village in great force, having before it a ravine which formed its position.

The Emperor reconnoitred the strength and the position of the enemy, and resolved to attack immediately. It became necessary to change front, the right in advance, and pivoting upon Fleurus.

General Vandamme marched upon St. Amand, General Girard upon Ligny, and Marshal Grouchy upon Sombref. The 4th division of the 2nd corps, commanded by General Girard, marched in reserve behind the corps of General Vandamme. The guard was drawn up on the heights of Fleurus, as well as the cuirassiers of General Milhaud.

At three in the afternoon, these dispositions were finished The division of General Lefol, forming part of the corps of General Vandamme, was first engaged, and made itself master of St. Amand, whence it drove out the enemy at the point of the bayonet. It kept its ground during the whole of the engagement, at the burial-ground and steeple of St. Amand: but that village, which is very extensive, was the theatre of various combats during the evening; the whole corps of Gen. Vandamme was there engaged, and the enemy there fought in considerable force.

General Girard, placed as a reserve to the corps of General Vandamme, turned the village by its right, and fought there with his accustomed valour. The respective forces were supported on both sides by about 30 pieces of cannon each.

On the right, General Girard came into action with the 4th corps, at the village of Ligny, which was taken and retaken several times.

Marshal Grouchy, on the extreme right, and General Pajol fought at the village of Sombref. The enemy showed from 80,000 to 90,000 men, and a great number of cannon.

At seven o'clock we were masters of all the villages situate on the bank of the ravine, which covered the enemy's position; but he still occupied, with all his masses, the heights of the mill of Bossy.

The Emperor returned with his guard to the village of Ligny; General Girard directed General Pecheux to debouch with what remained of the reserves almost all the troops having been engaged in that village.

Eight battalions of the guard debouched with fixed bayonets, and behind them, four squadrons of the guards, the *cuirassiers* of General Delort, those of General Milhaud, and the grenadiers of the horse guards. The Old guard attacked with the bayonet the enemy's columns, which were on the heights of Bussy, and in an instant covered the field of battle with dead. The squadron of the guard attacked and broke a square, and the *cuirassiers* repulsed the enemy in all directions.

At half past nine o'clock we had forty pieces of cannon, several carriages, colours, and prisoners, and the enemy sought safety in a precipitate retreat. At ten o'clock the battle was finished, and we found ourselves masters of the field of battle.

General Lutzow, a partisan, was taken prisoner. The prisoners assure us, that Field Marshal Blücher was wounded. The flower of the Prussian army was destroyed in this battle. Its loss could not be less than 15,000 men. Ours was 3,000 killed and wounded.

On the left, Marshal Ney had marched on Quatre Bras with a division, which cut in pieces an English division which was stationed there: but being attacked by the Prince of Orange with 25 thousand men, partly English, partly Hanoverians in the pay of England, he retired upon, his position at Frasnes. There a multiplicity of combats took place, the enemy obstinately endeavoured to force it, but in vain. The Duke of Elchingen waited for the first corps, which did not arrive till night; he confined himself to maintaining his position.

In a square attacked by the 9th regiment of *Cuirassiers* the colours of the 60th regiment of English Infantry fell into our hands. The Duke of Brunswick was killed. The Prince of Orange has been wounded. We are assured that the enemy had many personages and generals of note killed or wounded; we estimate the loss of the English at from 4,000 to 5,000 men, ours on this side was very considerable; it amounts to 4,200 killed or wounded. The combat ended with the approach of night Lord Wellington then evacuated Quatre Bras, and proceeded to Genappes.

In the morning of the 17th, the Emperor repaired to Quatre Bras, whence he marched to attack the English army: he drove it to the entrance of the forest of Soignes with the left wing and the reserve. The right wing advanced by Sombref, in pursuit of Field-Marshal Blücher, who was going towards Wavre, where he appeared to wish to take a position.

At ten o'clock in the evenings the English army occupied Mont St. Jean with its centre, and was in position before the forest of Soignes: it would have required three hours to attack it, we were therefore obliged to postpone it till the next day.

The headquarters of the Emperor were established at the farm of Oaillon, near Planchenoit, The rain fell in torrents. Thus, on the 16th, the left wing, the right, and the reserve, were equally engaged, at a distance of about two leagues.

Battle of Mont St. Jean.—At nine in the morning, the rain having somewhat abated, the 1st corps put itself in motion, and placed itself with the left on the road to Brussels, and opposite the village of Mont St. Jean, which appeared the centre of the enemy's position. The 3rd corps leaned its right upon the road to Brussels, and its left upon a small wood, within cannon shot of the English army. The *cuirassiers* were in reserve behind, and the guard in reserve upon the heights.

The 6th corps, with the cavalry of General D'Aumont, under the orders of Count Lobau, was destined to proceed in rear of our right to oppose a Prussian corps, which appeared to have escaped Marshal Grouchy, and to intend to fall upon our right flank, an intention which had been made known to us by our reports, and by the letter of a Prussian general, inclosing an order of battle, and which was taken by our light troops.

The troops were full of ardour. We estimated the force of the English army at 80,000 men. We supposed that the Prussian corps, which might be in line towards the right, might be 15,000 men. The enemy's force, then, was upwards of 90,000 men, ours less numerous.

At noon, all the preparations being terminated, Prince Jerome, commanding a division of the second corps, and destined to form the extreme left of it, advanced upon the wood of which the enemy occupied a part. The cannonade began. The enemy supported, with 30 pieces of cannon, the troops he had sent to keep the wood. We made also on our side dispositions of artillery. At one o'clock, Prince Jerome was master of all the wood, and the whole English army fell back behind a curtain. Count d'Erlon then attacked the village of Mont St. Jean, and supported his attack with 80 pieces of cannon, which must have occasioned great loss to the English army.

All the efforts were made towards the ridge. A brigade of the 1st division of Count d'Erlon took the village of Mont St. Jean, a second brigade was charged by a corps of English cavalry, which occasioned it much loss. At the same moment, a division of English cavalry, charged the battery of Count d'Erlon by its right, and disorganised several pieces; but the *cuirassiers* of general Milhaud charged that division, three regiments of which were broken and cut up.

It was three in the afternoon. The Emperor made the guard advance to place it in the plain upon the ground which the first corps had occupied at the outset of the battle; this corps being already in advance. The Prussian division, whose movement had been foreseen, then engaged with the light troops of Count Lobau, spreading its fire upon our whole right flank. It was expedient, before undertaking anything elsewhere, to wait for the event of this attack. Hence, all the means in reserve were ready to succour Count Lobau, and overwhelm the Prussian corps when it should be advanced.

This done, the Emperor had the design of leading an attack upon the village of Mont St Jean, from which we expected decisive success; but, by a movement of impatience so frequent in our military annals, and, which has often been so fatal to us, the cavalry of reserve, having perceived a retrograde movement made by the English to shelter themselves from our batteries, from which they suffered so much, crowned the heights of Mont St Jean, and charged the infantry. This movement, which, made in time, and supported by the reserves, must have decided the day, made in an isolated manner, and before affairs on the right were terminated, became fatal.

Having no means of countermanding it, the enemy shewing many masses of cavalry and infantry, and our two divisions of *cuirassiers* being engaged, all our cavalry ran at the same moment to support their comrades. There, for three hours numerous charges were made, which enabled us to penetrate several squares, and to take six standards of the light infantry, an advantage out of proportion with the Joss which our cavalry experienced by the grape-shot and musket-firing. It was impossible to dispose of our reserves of infantry until we had repulsed the flank attack of the Prussian corps. This attack always prolonged itself perpendicularly upon our right flank.

The Emperor sent thither General Duhesme with the young guard, and several batteries of reserve. The enemy was kept in check, repulsed, fend fell back—he had exhausted his forces, and we had. nothing to fear. It was this moment that was indicated for an attack upon the centre of the enemy. As the *cuirassiers* suffered by the grape-shot, we sent four battalions of the middle guard to protect the *cuirassiers*, keep the position, and, if possible, disengage end draw back into toe plain a part of our cavalry.

Two other battalions were sent to keep themselves *en potence* upon the extreme left of the division, which had manoeuvred upon our flanks, in order not to have any uneasiness on that side—the rest was disposed in reserve, part to occupy the *potence*

95

in rear of Mont St Jean, part upon the ridge in rear of the field of battle, which formed out position of retreat.

In this state of affairs, the battle was gained; we occupied all the positions, which the enemy occupied at the outset of the battle: our cavalry having been too soon and ill employed, we could no longer hope for decisive success; but Marshal Grouchy, having learned the movement of the Prussian corps, marched upon the rear of that corps, which insured us a signal success for next day. After eight hours' fire and charges of infantry and cavalry, all the army saw with joy the battle gained, and the field of battle in our power.

At half-past eight o'clock, the four battalions of the middle guard, who had been sent to the ridge on the other side of Mont St. Jean in order to support the *cuirassiers*, bring greatly annoyed by the grape-shot, endeavoured to carry the batteries with the bayonet At the end of the day, a charge directed against their flank, by several English squadrons, put them in disorder. The fugitives re-crossed the ravine. Several regiments, near at hand, seeing some troops belonging to the guard in confusion, believed it was the old guard, and in consequence were thrown into disorder.

Cries of '*all is lost, the guard is driven back*', were heard on every side. The soldiers pretend even that on many points ill disposed persons cried out, '*sauve qui peut*', However this may be, a complete panic at once spread itself throughout the whole field of battle, and they threw themselves in the greatest disorder on the line of communication; soldiers, caanoneers, *caissons*, all pressed to this point; the old guard, which was in reserve, was infected, and was itself hurried along.

In an instant, the whole army was nothing but a mass of confusion; all the soldiers, of all arms, were mixed *pêle mêle*, and it was utterly impossible to rally a single corps. The enemy, who perceived this astonishing confusion, immediately attacked with their cavalry, and increased the disorder; and such was the confusion, owing to night coming on, that it was impossible to rally the troops, and point out to them their error. Thus a battle terminated, a day of false manoeuvres rectified, the greatest success insured for the next day, all was lost by a moment of panic terror.

Even the squadrons of *service* drawn up by the side of the Emperor were overthrown and disorganised by these tumultuous waves, and there was then nothing else to be done but to follow the torrent. The parks of reserve, the baggage which had not repassed the Sambre, in short everything that was on the field of battle, remained in the power of the enemy. It was impossible to wait for the troops on our right; everyone knows what the bravest army in the world is when thus mixed and thrown into confusion, and when its organization no longer exists.

The Emperor crossed the Sambre at Charleroi, at five o'clock in the morning of the 19th. Philippeville and Avesnes have been given as the points of reunion. Prince Jerome, General Morand, and other generals, have there already rallied a part of the army. Marshal Grouchy, with the corps on the right, is moving on the Lower Sambre.

The loss of the enemy must have been very great, if we may judge from the number of standards we have taken from them, and from the retrograde movements which he made;—ours cannot be calculated till after the troops shall have been collected. Before the disorder broke out, we had already experienced a very considerable loss, particularly in our cavalry, so fatally, though so bravely engaged.

Notwithstanding these losses, this brave cavalry constantly kept the position it had taken from the English, and only abandoned it when the tumult and disorder of the field of battle forced it. In the midst of the night, and the obstacles which encumbered their route, it could not preserve its own organization.

The artillery has, as usual, covered itself with glory. The carriages belonging to the headquarters remained in their ordinary position: no retrograde movement being judged necessary. In the course of the night they fell into the enemy's hands.

Such has been the issue of the battle of Mont St. Jean, glorious for the French armies, and yet so fatal.

4. MARSHAL NEY'S ACCOUNT.

THE PRINCE OF MOSKWA (MARSHAL NEY) TO HIS EXCELLENCY THE DUKE OF OTRANTO.

M. le Duc,—The most false and defamatory reports have been spreading for some days over the public mind, upon the conduct which I have pursued during this short and unfortunate campaign. The journals have reported those odious calumnies, and appear to lend them credit. After having fought for twenty-five years for my country, after having shed my blood for its glory and independence, an attempt is made to accuse me of treason; an attempt is made to mark me out to the people and the army itself, as the author of the disaster it has just experienced.

Forced to break silence, while it is always painful to speak ,of oneself, and above all, to answer calumnies, I address myself to you, Sir, as the President of the Provisional Government, for the purpose of laying before you a faithful statement of the events I have witnessed. On the 11th of June, I received an order from the Minister of War to repair to the Imperial presence. I had no command, and no information upon the composition and strength of the army.

Neither the Emperor nor his Minister had given me any previous hint, from which I could anticipate that I should be employed in the present campaign, I was consequently taken by surprise, without horse, without accoutrements, and without money, and I was obliged to borrow the necessary expenses of my journey. Having arrived on the 12th, at Laon, on the 13th at Avesnes, and on the 14th at Beaumont, I purchased, in this last city, two horses from the Duke of Treviso, with which I repaired, on the 15th, to Charleroi, accompanied by my first *aide-de-camp*, the only officer who attended me. I arrived at the moment when the enemy, attacked by our troops, was retreating upon Fleurus and Gosselies.

The Emperor ordered me immediately to put myself at the head of the 1st and 2nd corps of infantry, commanded by Lieutenant-Generals d'Erlon and Reille, of the divisions of light cavalry of Lieutenant-General Pine, of the division of light cavalry of the guards, under the command of Lieutenant-Generals Lefebvre Desnouettes and Colbert, and of two divisions of cavalry of the Count Valmy, forming, in all, eight divisions of infantry, and four of cavalry.

With these troops, a part of which only I had as yet under my immediate command, I pursued the enemy, and forced him to evacuate Gosselies, Frasnes, Millet, Heppegnies. There they took up a position for the night, with the exception of the 1st corps, which was still at Marchiennes, and which did not join me till the following day.

On the 16th, I received orders to attack the English in their position at Quatre Bras. We advanced towards the enemy with an enthusiasm difficult to be described. Nothing resisted our impetuosity The battle became general, and victory was no longer doubtful, when, at the moment that I intended to order up the first corps of infantry, which had been left by me in reserve at Frasnes, I learned that the Emperor had disposed of it without adverting me of the circumstance, as well as of the division of Girard of the second corps, on purpose to direct them upon St. Amand, and to strengthen his left wing, which was vigorously engaged with the Prussians.

The shock which this intelligence gave me, confounded me. Having no longer under me more than three divisions, instead of the eight upon which I calculated, I was obliged to renounce the hopes of victory; and, in spite of all my efforts, in spite of the intrepidity and devotion of my troops, my utmost efforts after that could only maintain me in my position till the close of the day.

About nine o'clock, the first corps was sent me by the Emperor, to whom it had been of no service. Thus twenty-five or thirty thousand men were, I may say, paralysed, and were idly paraded during the whole of the battle from the right to the left, and the left to the right, without firing a shot.

It is impossible for me, Sir, not to arrest your attention for a moment upon these details, in order to bring before your view all the consequences of this false movement, and in general, of the bad arrangements during the whole of the day. By what fatality, for example did the Emperor, instead of leading all his forces against Lord Wellington, who would have been attacked unawares, and could not have resisted, consider this attack as secondary? How did the Emperor, after the passage of the Sambre, conceive it possible to fight. two battles on the same day? It was to oppose forces double ours, and to do what military men who were witnesses of it can scarcely yet comprehend.

Instead of this, had he left a corps of observation to watch the Prussians, and marched with his most powerful masses to support me, the English army had undoubtedly been destroyed between Quatre Bras, and Genappes; and this position, which separated the two allied armies, being once in our power, would have opened for the Emperor an opportunity of advancing to the right of the Prussians, and of crushing them in their turn. The general opinion in France and especially in the army, was, that the Emperor would have bent his whole efforts to annihilate first the English army; and circumstances were favourable for the accomplishment of such a project: but fate ordered otherwise.

On the 17th, the army marched in the direction of Mont St. Jean.

On the 18th, the battle began at one o'clock, and though the bulletin, which details it, makes no mention of me, it is not necessary for me to mention that I was engaged in it. Lieutenant-General Count Drouet has already spoken of that battle, in the House of Peers. His narration is accurately with the exception of some important facts which he has passed over in silence, or of which he was ignorant, and which it is now my duty to declare.

About seven o'clock in the evening, after the most frightful carnage which I have ever witnessed, General Labedoyere came to me with a message from the Emperor, that Marshal Grouchy had arrived an our right, and attacked the left of the English and Prussians united. This General Officer, in riding along the lines, spread this intelligence among the soldiers, whose courage and devotion remained unshaken, and who gave new proofs of them at that moment, in spite of the fatigue which they experienced.

Immediately after, what was my astonishment, I should rather say indignation, when I learned that so far from Marshal Grouchy having arrived to support us, as the whole army had been assured, between forty and fifty thousand Prussians attached our extreme right, and forced it to retire!

Whether the Emperor was deceived with regard to the time when the Marshal could support him, or whether the march of the Marshal was retarded by the efforts of the enemy longer than was calculated upon, the fact is, that at the moment when his arrival was announced to us, he was only at Wavre upon the Dyle, which to us was the same as if he had been 800 leagues from the field of battle.

A short time afterwards, I saw four regiments of the middle guard, conducted by the Emperor, arriving. With these troops he wished to renew the attack, and to penetrate the centre of the enemy. He orered me to lead them on; generals, officers, and soldiers, all displayed the greatest intrepidity; but this body of troops was too weak to resist for a long time, the forces opposed to it by the enemy, and it was soon necessary to renounce the hope which this attack had, for a few moments, inspired. General Friant had been struck with a ball by my side, and I myself had my horse killed, and fell under it.

The brave men who will return from this terrible battle, will, I hope, do me the justice to say, that they saw me on foot with sword in hand during the whole of the evening, and that I only quitted the scene of carnage among the last, and at the moment when retreat could no longer be prevented. At the same time, the Prussians continued their offensive movements, and our right sensibly retired, the English advancing in their turn. There remained to us still four squares of the Old Guard to protect the retreat These brave grenadiers, the choice of the army, forced successively to retire, yielded ground foot by foot, till, overwhelmed by numbers, they were almost entirely annihilated.

From that moment a retrograde movement was declared, and the army formed nothing but a confused mass. There was not, however, a total rout, nor the cry of '*sauve qui peut*', as has been calumniously stated in the bulletin. As for myself, constantly in the rear guard, which I followed on foot, having all my horses killed, worn out with fatigue, covered with contusions, and having no longer strength to march, I owe my life to a corporal who supported me on the road, and did not abandon me during the retreat.

At eleven at night I found Lieutenant-General Lefebvre Desnouettes, and one of his officers, Major Schmidt, had the generosity to give me the only horse that remained to him. In this manner I arrived at Marchienne-au-pont at four o'clock in the morning, alone, without any officers of my staff, ignorant of what had become of the Emperor, who, before the end of the battle, had entirely disappeared, and who, I was allowed to believe, might be either killed or taken, prisoner.

General Pamphele Lacroix, chief of the staff of the second corps, whom I found in this city, having told me that the Emperor was at Charleroi, I was led to suppose that His Majesty was going to put himself at the head of Marshal Grouchy's corps, to cover the Sambre, and to facilitate to the troops the means of rallying towards Avesnes, and, with this persuasion, I went to Beaumont: but parties of cavalry following on the near, and having already intercepted the roads of Maubeuge and Philippeville, I became sensible of the total impossibility of arresting a single soldier to oppose the progress of the victorious enemy. I continued my march upon Avesnes, where I could obtain no intelligence of what had become of the Emperor.

In this state of matters, having no knowledge of His Majesty, nor of the Major-General, confusion increasing every moment, and, with the exception of some fragments of the guard and of the line, every one following his own inclination, I determined immediately to go to Paris by St, Quentin, to disclose, as quickly as possible, the true state of affairs to the Minister of War, that he might send to the army some fresh troops, and take the measures which circumstances rendered necessary. At my arrival at Bourget, three leagues from Paris, I learned that the Emperor had passed there at nine o'clock in the morning.

Such, M, le Duc, is a history of the calamitous campaign

Now, I ask those who have survived this fine and numerous army, how I can be accused of the disasters of which it has been the victim, and of which your military annals furnish no example. I have, it is said, betrayed my country,—I who, to serve it, have shewn a zeal which I perhaps have carried to an extravagant height; but this calumny is supported by no fact, by no circumstance. But how can these odious reports, which spread with frightful rapidity, be arrested?

If, in the researches which I could make on this subject, I did not fear almost as much to discover as to be ignorant of the truth, I would say, that all has a tendency to convince, that I have been unworthily deceived, and that it is attempted to cover with the pretence of treason, the faults and extravagancies of this campaign—faults which have not yet been avowed in the bulletins which have appeared, and against which I in vain raised that voice of truth which I will yet cause to resound in the House of Peers. I expect, from the candour of your Excellency, and from your indulgence to me, that you will cause this letter to be inserted in the *Journals*, and give it the greatest possible publicity.

I renew to your Excellency, &c.

Paris, June 26, 1815.   Marshal Prince of Moskwa.

5. MARSHAL GROUCHY'S ACCOUNT.

REPORT ADDRESSED TO THE EMPEROR BY MARSHAL DE GROUCHY.

Dinant, June 20th, 1815.—It was not till after seven in the evening of the 18th of June, that I received the letter of the Duke of Dalmatia, which directed me to march on St Lambert, and to attack General Bulow. I fell in with the enemy as I was marching on Wavre. He was immediately driven into Wavre, and General Vandamme's corps attacked that town, and was warmly engaged. The portion of Wavre, on the right of the Dyle, was carried, but much difficulty was experienced in debouching on the other side. General Girard was wounded by a ball in the breast while endeavouring to carry the mill of Bielge, in order to pass the river, but in which he did not succeed, and Lieutenant-General Aix had been killed in the attack on the town.

In this state of things, being impatient to co-operate with your Majesty's army on that important day, I detached several corps to force the passage of the Dyle and march against Bulow.

The corps of Vandamme, in the meantime, maintained the attack on Wavre, and on the mill, whence the enemy showed an intention to debouch, but which I did not conceive he was capable of effecting. I arrived at Limale, passed the river, and the heights were carried by the division of Vichery and the cavalry. Night did not permit us to advance farther, and I no longer heard the cannon on the side where your Majesty was engaged.

I halted in this situation until daylight. Wavre and Bielge were occupied by the Prussians, who, at three in the morning of the 18th, attacked in their turn, wishing to take advantage of the difficult position in which I was, and expecting to drive me into the defile, and take the artillery which had debouched, and make me repass the Dyle. Their efforts were fruitless. The Prussians were repulsed, and the village of Bielge taken. The brave General Penny was killed.

General Vandamme then passed one of his divisions by Bielge, and carried with ease the heights of Wavre, and along the whole of my line the success was complete. I was in front of Rozierne, preparing to march on Brussels, when I received the sad intelligence of the loss of the Battle of Waterloo. The officer who brought it informed me, that your Majesty was retreating on the Sambre, without being able to indicate any particular point on which I should direct my march. I ceased to pursue, and began my retrograde movement. The retreating enemy did not think of following me.

Learning that the enemy had already passed the Sambre, and was on my flank, and not being sufficiently strong to make a diversion in favour of your Majesty, without compromising that which I commanded, I marched on Namur. At this moment, the rear of the columns were attacked. That of the left made a retrograde movement sooner than was expected, which endangered, for a moment, the retreat of the left; but good dispositions soon repaired everything, and two pieces which had been, taken were recovered by the brave 20th Dragoons, who besides took an howitzer from the enemy.

We entered Namur without loss. The long defile which extends from this place to Dinant, in which only a single column can march, and the embarrassment arising from the numerous transports of wounded rendered: it necessary to hold for a considerable time the town, in which I had not the means of blowing up the bridge. I entrusted the defence of Namur to General Vandamme, who, with his usual intrepidity maintained himself there till eight in the evening; so that nothing was left behind, and I occupied Dinant

The enemy has lost some thousands of men in the attack on Namur, where the contest was very obstinate; the troops, have performed their duty in a manner worthy of praise.

(Signed)   De Grouchy.

PRIVATE FRENCH LETTERS.

*June 17,*1915—The French armies have again immortalized themselves on the plains of Fleurus.

We entered Belgium on the 15th, The enemy was overthrown in a first affair upon every point where he attempted to, resist us.

Before Charleroi, several of his squares were broken and taken by some squadrons only: one thousand seven hundred prisoners only could be saved out of five or six thousand men who composed these squares. Yesterday (the 16th) we encountered the whole of the enemy's army, in its position near Fleurus; its right, composed of English, under the command of Wellington, was in front of Meller, its centre at St. Amand, and its left at Sombref, a formidable position, covered by the little River Ligny.

The enemy occupied also the little village of Ligny, in front of this river. Our army debouched in the plain, its left under Marshal Ney, by Gosselies, the centre where the Emperor Was, by Fleurus, and the right under General Girard, upon Sombref. The actions began at two o'clock upon the left and centre. Both sides fought with inconceivable fury.

The villages of St. Amand and Ligny were taken and retaken four times. Our soldiers have all covered themselves with glory. At eight o'clock the Emperor, with his whole guard, had Ligny attacked and carried. Our brave fellows advanced at the first discharge upon the principal position of the enemy. His army was forced in the centre, and obliged to retreat in the greatest disorder; Blücher with the Prussians, upon Namur, and Wellington upon Brussels.

Several pieces of cannon were taken by the guard, who bore down all before them. All march with cries a thousand times repeated of "*Vive l'Empereur!*" These were also the last words of the brave men who fell. Never was such enthusiasm; a British division of five or six thousand Scottish was cut to pieces; we have not seen any of them prisoners. The Noble Lord must be confounded. There were upon the field of battle eight enemies to one Frenchman. Their lost is said to be fifty thousand men. The cannonade was like that at the Battle of the Moskwa.

This morning (the 17th) the cavalry of General Pajol is gone in pursuit of the Prussians upon the road to Namur. It is already two leagues and a half in advance; whole bands of prisoners are taken. They do not know what is become of their commanders. The rout is complete on our side, and I hope we shall not so soon hear again of the Prussians, if they should ever be able to rally at all.

As for the English, we shall see now what will become of them. The Emperor is here.

Some private letters from the army give the following particulars:—

The English are retiring upon Brussels by the Forest of Soignes; the Prussians are falling back upon the Meuse in great disorder.

The 17th at 11 p.m. the Emperor had his headquarters at Planchenoit, a village only five leagues from Brussels. The rain fell in torrents. His Majesty was fatigued, but he was very well.

Count Lobau, who was marching with the 6th corps upon

Namur, was, with his vanguard, only half a league from the town. Five battalions are gone from Lille to escort the prisoners taken on the 15th and 16th.

6 DUKE OF WELLINGTON'S ACCOUNT

LONDON GAZETTE EXTRAORDINARY, JUNE 22ND.

Downing-street, June 22nd, 1815.—Major the Honourable H. Perey. arrived last night with a dispatch from Field Marshal the Duke of Wellington, K. G. to Earl Bathurst, his Majesty's Principal Secretary of State for the War Department, of which the following is a copy:

Waterloo, June, 19th, 1815.

My Lord,—Buonaparte having collected the 1st, 2nd, 3rd, 4th, and 6th, corps of the French army and the Imperial Guards, and nearly all the cavalry, on the Sambre, and between that river and the Meuse, between the 10th and 14th of the month, advanced on the 15th and attacked the Prussian posts at Thuin and Lobez, on the Sambre, at daylight in the morning.

I did not hear of these events till the evening of the 15th, and I immediately ordered the troops to prepare to march; and afterwards to march to the left, as soon as I had intelligence from other quarters to prove that the enemy's movement upon Charleroi was the real attack.

The enemy drove the Prussian posts from the Sambre on that day; and General Ziethen, who commanded the corps which had been at Charleroi, retired upon Fleurus; and Marshal Prince Blücher concentrated the Prussian army upon Sombref, holding the villages in front of his position of St. Amand and Ligny.

The enemy continued his march along the road from Charleroi towards Brussels, and on the same evening, the 15th, attacked a brigade of the army of the Netherlands, under Prince de Weimar, posted at Frasne, and forced it back to the farmhouse on the same road, called Les Quatre Bras.

The Prince of Orange immediately reinforced this brigade with another of the same division, under General Perponcher, and, in the morning early, regained part of the ground which had been lost, so as to have the command of the communication leading from Nivelles and Brussels, with Marshal Blücher's position.

In the meantime, I had directed the whole army to march upon Les Quatre Bras, and the 5th division, under Lieutenant-General Sir Thomas Picton, arrived at about half past two in the day, followed by the corps of troops under the Duke of Brunswick, and afterwards by the contingent of Nassau.

At this time the enemy commenced an attack upon Prince Blücher with his whole force, excepting the 1st and 2nd corps; and a corps of cavalry under General Kellerman, with which he attacked our post at Les Quatre Bras.

The Prussian army maintained their position with their utmost gallantry and perseverance, against a great disparity of numbers, as the 4th corps of their army, under General Bulow, had not joined, and I was not able to assist them as I wished, as I was attacked myself, and the troops, the cavalry in particular, which had a long distance to march, had not arrived.

We maintained our position also, and completely defeated and repulsed all the enemy's attempts to get possession of it. The enemy repeatedly attacked us with a large body of infantry and cavalry, supported by a numerous and powerful artillery; he made several charges with the cavalry upon out infantry, but all were repulsed in the steadiest manner.

In this affair, his Royal Highness the Prince of Orange, the Duke of Brunswick, and Lieutenant-General Sir Thomas Picton, and Major-General Sir James Kempt, and Sir Denis Pack, who were engaged from the commencement of the enemy's attack, highly distinguished themselves, as well as Lieutenant-General Charles Baron Alten, Major-

General Sir C. Halket, Lieutenant-General Cooke, and Major-Generals Maitland and Byng, as they successively arrived.

The troops of the 5th division, and those of the Brunswick corps, were long and severely engaged, and conducted themselves with the utmost gallantry. I must particularly mention the 28th, 42nd, 78th, and 92nd regiments, and the battalion of Hanoverians.

Our loss was great; as your Lordship will perceive by the inclosed return; and I have particularly to regret His Serene Highness the Duke of Brunswick, who fell, fighting gallantly at the head of his troops.

Although Marshal Blücher had maintained his position at Sombref, he still found himself much weakened by the severity of the contest in which he had been engaged, and, as the 4th corps had not arrived, he determined to fall back, and concentrated his army upon Wavre; and he marched in the night after the action was over.

This movement of the Marshal's rendered necessary a corresponding one on my part; and I retired from the farm of Quatre Bras upon Genappe, and thence upon Waterloo the next morning, the 17th, at ten o'clock.

The enemy made no effort to pursue Marshal Blücher. On the contrary, a *patrole* which I sent to Sombref, in the morning, found all quiet, and the enemy's *videttes* fell back as the *patrole* advanced. Neither did he attempt to molest our march to the rear, although made in the middle of the day, excepting by following with a large body of cavalry, (brought from his right) the cavalry under the Earl of Ux bridge.

This gave Lord Uxbridge an opportunity of charging them with the 1st Life Guards, upon their debouche from the village of Genappe, upon which occasion his Lordship has declared himself to be well satisfied with that regiment.

The position which I took up, in front of Waterloo, crossed

the high roads from Charleroi and Nivelles, and had its right thrown back to a ravine near Merke Braine, which was occupied, and its left extended to a height above the hamlet Ter la Haye, which was likewise occupied.

In front of the right centre, and near the Nivelle road, we occupied the house and garden of Hougoumont, which covered the return of that flank; and in front of the left centre, we occupied the farm of La Haye Sainte. By our left we communicated with Marshal Prince Blücher, at Wavre, through Ohain, and the Marshal had promised me, that in case we should be attacked, he would support me with one or more corps, as might be necessary.

The enemy collected his army, with the exception of the third corps which had been sent to observe Marshal Blücher, on a range of heights in our front, in the course of the night of the 17th and yesterday morning; and at about ten o'clock he commenced a furious attack upon our post at Hougoumont. I had occupied that post with a detachment from General Byng's brigade of Guards, which was in position in its rear; and it was for some time under the command of Lieutenant Colonel Macdonald, and afterwards of Colonel Home; and I am happy to add, that it was maintained, throughout the day, with the utmost gallantry by these brave troops, notwithstanding the repeated efforts of large bodies of the enemy to obtain possession of it.

This attack upon the right of our centre was accompanied by a very heavy cannonade upon our whole line, which was destined to support the repealed attacks of cavalry and infantry occasionally mixed, but sometimes separate, which were made upon it. In one of these, the enemy carried the farmhouse of La Haye Sainte, as the detachment of the light battalion of the legion which occupied it had expended all its ammunition, and the enemy occupied the only communication there was with them.

The enemy repeatedly charged our infantry with his cavalry; but these attacks were uniformly unsuccessful, and they afforded opportunities to our cavalry to charge, in one of which, Lord E. Somerset's brigade, Royal Horse Guards, and 1st Dragoon Guards, highly distinguished themselves; as did that of Major-General Sir W. Ponsonby, having taken many prisoners and an eagle.

These attacks were repeated till about seven in the evening, when the enemy made a desperate effort with the cavalry and infantry, to force our left centre, near the farm of La Haye Sainte, which, after a severe contest, was defeated; and having observed that the troops retired from the attack in great confusion, and that the march of General Bulow's corps by Frichermont upon Planchenoit and *La Belle Alliance* had begun to take effect; and as I could perceive the fire of his cannon, and as Marshal Prince Blücher had joined in person, with a corps of his army to the left of our line by Ohain, I determined to attack the enemy, and immediately advanced the whole line of infantry, supported by the cavalry and artillery. The attack succeeded in every point; the enemy was forced from his position on the heights, and fled in the utmost confusion, leaving behind him, as far as I can judge, *one hundred and fifty pieces of cannon*, with their ammunition, which fell into our hands. I continued the pursuit till long after dark, and then discontinued it only on account of the fatigue of our troops, who had been engaged during twelve hours, and because I found myself on the same road with Marshal Blücher, who assured me of his intention to follow the enemy throughout the night: he has sent me word this morning that he had taken 60 pieces of cannon belonging to the Imperial Guard, and several carriages, baggage, &c. belonging to Buonaparte, in Genappe.

I propose to move this morning upon Nivelles, and not to discontinue my operation.

Your Lordship will observe, that such a desperate action could not be fought, and such advantages could not be gained, without great loss; and I am sorry to add that ours has been immense. In Lieutenant-General Sir Thomas Picton, His Majesty has sustained the loss of an officer who has frequently distinguished himself in his service; and he fell gloriously leading his division to a charge with bayonets, by which one of the most serious attacks made by the enemy on our position was defeated.

The Earl of Uxbridge, after having successfully got through this arduous day, received a wound, by almost the last shot fired, which will, I am afraid, deprive His Majesty for some time of his services.

His Royal Highness the Prince of Orange distinguished himself by his gallantry and conduct till be received a wound from a musket-ball, through the shoulder, which obliged him to quit the field.

It gives me the greatest satisfaction to assure your Lordship, that the army never, upon any occasion, conducted itself better. The division of Guards, under Lieutenant-General Cooke, who is severely wounded, Major-General Maitland and Major Byng, set an example which was followed by all; and there is no officer, nor description of troops, that did not behave well.

I must, however, particularly mention, for His Royal Highness's approbation, Lieutenant-General Sir H. Clinton, Major-General Adam, Lieutenant-General Charles Baron Alten, severely wounded; Major-General Sir Colin Halket, severely wounded; Colonel Ompteda, Colonel Mitchael, commanding a brigade of the 4th division; Major-General Sir James Kempt and Sir Denis Pack, Major-General Lambert, Major-General Lord E. Somerset, Major-General Sir W. Ponsonby, Major-General Sir C. Grant, and Major General Sir H. Vivian; Major-General Sir O. Vandeleur; Major-General Count Dornberg. I am also particularly indebted to General Lord Hill for his assistance and conduct upon this, as upon all former occasions.

The artillery and engineer departments were conducted

much to my satisfaction by Colonel Sir G; Wood, and Colonel Smyth; and I had every reason to be satisfied with the conduct of the Adjutant-General, Maj.-General Barnes, who was wounded, and of the Quarter-Master-General, Colonel Delancey, who was killed by a cannon shot in the middle of the action. This officer is a serious loss to His Majesty's service, and to me at this moment.

I was likewise much indebted to the assistance of Lieutenant-Colonel Lord Fitzroy Somerset, who was severely wounded, and of the officers composing my personal staff, who have suffered severely in this action. Lieutenant-Colonel the Honourable Sir Alexander Gordon, who has died of his wounds, was a most promising officer, and is a serious lost to His Majesty's service.

General Kruse, of the Nassau service, likewise conducted himself much to my satisfaction, as did General Trip, commandingthe heavy brigade of cavalry, and General Vanhope, commanding a brigade of infantry of the King of the Netherlands.

General Pozzo di Borgo, General Baron Vincent, General Muffling, and General Alava, were in the field during the action, and rendered me every assistance in their power. Baron Vincent is wounded, but I hope not severely; and General Pozzo di Borgo received a contusion.

I should not do justice to my feelings, or to Marshal Blücher and the Prussian army, if I did not attribute the successful result of this arduous day to the cordial and timely assistance received from them.

The operation of General Bulow upon the enemy's flank was a most decisive one; and, even if I had not found myself in a situation to make the attack, which produced the final result, it would have forced the enemy to retire, if his attacks should have failed, and would have prevented him from taking advantage of them, if they should unfortunately have succeeded.

I send, with this dispatch, two eagles, taken by the troops

in this action, which Major Percy will have the honour of laying at the feet of his Royal Highness—I beg leave to recommend him to your lordship's protection.

I have the honour, &c.

(Signed)   Wellington.

LEONAUR

ALSO FROM LEONAUR
AVAILABLE IN SOFTCOVER OR HARDCOVER WITH DUST JACKET

FARAWAY CAMPAIGN *by F. James*—Experiences of an Indian Army Cavalry Officer in Persia & Russia During the Great War.

REVOLT IN THE DESERT *by T. E. Lawrence*—An account of the experiences of one remarkable British officer's war from his own perspective.

MACHINE-GUN SQUADRON *by A. M. G.*—The 20th Machine Gunners from British Yeomanry Regiments in the Middle East Campaign of the First World War.

A GUNNER'S CRUSADE *by Antony Bluett*—The Campaign in the Desert, Palestine & Syria as Experienced by the Honourable Artillery Company During the Great War .

DESPATCH RIDER *by W. H. L. Watson*—The Experiences of a British Army Motorcycle Despatch Rider During the Opening Battles of the Great War in Europe.

TIGERS ALONG THE TIGRIS *by E. J. Thompson*—The Leicestershire Regiment in Mesopotamia During the First World War.

HEARTS & DRAGONS *by Charles R. M. F. Crutwell*—The 4th Royal Berkshire Regiment in France and Italy During the Great War, 1914-1918.

INFANTRY BRIGADE: 1914 *by John Ward*—The Diary of a Commander of the 15th Infantry Brigade, 5th Division, British Army, During the Retreat from Mons.

DOING OUR 'BIT' *by Ian Hay*—Two Classic Accounts of the Men of Kitchener's 'New Army' During the Great War including *The First 100,000* & *All In It*.

AN EYE IN THE STORM *by Arthur Ruhl*—An American War Correspondent's Experiences of the First World War from the Western Front to Gallipoli-and Beyond.

STAND & FALL *by Joe Cassells*—With the Middlesex Regiment Against the Bolsheviks 1918-19.

RIFLEMAN MACGILL'S WAR *by Patrick MacGill*—A Soldier of the London Irish During the Great War in Europe including *The Amateur Army, The Red Horizon* & *The Great Push*.

WITH THE GUNS *by C. A. Rose & Hugh Dalton*—Two First Hand Accounts of British Gunners at War in Europe During World War 1- Three Years in France with the Guns and With the British Guns in Italy.

THE BUSH WAR DOCTOR *by Robert V. Dolbey*—The Experiences of a British Army Doctor During the East African Campaign of the First World War.

www.ingramcontent.com/pod-product-compliance
Lightning Source LLC
Chambersburg PA
CBHW031900090426
42741CB00005B/576